A SOFT PLACE TO LAND

By

Michelle Alden

A Soft Place to Land

Copyright © 2014 Michelle Alden

All rights reserved

Published 2014.

No part of this publication may be reproduced, distributed, or transmitted in any form or by any means, including photocopying, recording, or other electronic or mechanical methods, without the prior written permission of the publisher, except in the case of brief quotations embodied in critical reviews and certain other noncommercial uses permitted by copyright law. For permission requests, write to the publisher, addressed "Attention: Permissions Coordinator," at the address below.

First published by Faith Books & MORE

ISBN 978-1-939761-17-0

Printed in the United States of America
This book is printed on acid-free paper.

3255 Lawrenceville-Suwanee Rd. | Suite P250
Suwanee, GA 30024
publishing@faithbooksandmore.com
faithbooksandmore.com

Ordering Information:

Quantity sales. Special discounts are available on quantity purchases by corporations, associations, and others. For details, contact the publisher at the address above.

Orders by U.S. trade bookstores and wholesalers. Please contact Ingram Book Company: Tel: (800) 937-8000; Email: orders@ingrambook.com or visit ipage.ingrambook.com.

Disclaimer

The purpose of this book is to empower, educate, and offer hope. The authors of the book achieved that through their own experiences, expertise, and research. Consequently, this book should only be used as a road map. This book is not intended to be nor is it represented as legal advice. The authors are not liable or responsible, to any person, or entity, for any and all claims, demands, damages causes of action, suits in equity of whatever kind or nature, caused or alleged to have been caused, directly or indirectly, by the information contained in this book or the authors' past or future negligence or wrongful acts.

DEDICATION

For my son Nathan.

I am so thankful for you. I hope you know, no matter how grown-up you are, that you can always come home.

I pray that our family will always be a safe place to land.

ACKNOWLEDGEMENTS AND AUTHOR NOTES

This is my third book about the Keyton family and, like my readers, I have grown quite fond of them. When I write I am surprised at the places the characters take me. I have learned to go with them and enjoy the journey. I am thankful for TJ, Rachel and all the others that have come alive to me over the past few years. Their stories have helped me process different paths for my own family and our relationships. As I finish A SOFT PLACE TO LAND I am aware this is the final book about the Keytons—at least for now.

A little news from my own journey: An amazing thing happened as I was finishing my first two books. After 40 years, I was suddenly re-united with my birth family. I had just finished FROM THE INSIDE OUT, which I wrote to bring out real stories of adoption and abuse including some of my own childhood experiences. I planned all along to dedicate it to my two biological brothers because our adoption story started together. Within hours of signing an agreement with a publisher, my younger brother contacted me! As the books were being published my own adoption story was coming full circle. It's been several years now since that phone call. I am so happy to be connected with my roots. I am enjoying the new sense of belonging it has brought me and my children.

I want to thank my little brother Michael Bridge for his persistence in bringing us all together. I am so thankful for him and his family. Thanks, Casey, for encouraging him to keep looking for us! Mike also found our sister, Susan Volk, and her family. In my heart, I knew she was missing all along. I am thankful for the opportunity to know her now and look forward to more time together. My older brother, Jack, connected with our birth mother, Mike and me before he died. He did not get to see or read FROM THE INSIDE OUT. In the work I do for adoptive families and in my writing, he is close to my heart and usually on my mind.

Thank you to my birth mom, Kathy Hewitt, for making up for lost time and becoming such an important part of my life in these last few years. Thanks also for the absolute faith and confidence in me, and for helping to sell so many books! Kathy is my personal public relations person. If we ever get a movie out of SOUTHERN BLEND, I know you will be right there selling tickets! Thanks for believing in me! (Yes, my mom thinks I am special.)

Of course, I can't thank my amazing kids enough. Our family is changing in so many ways. During the time it has taken to write this third book, my oldest daughter, Bekah, graduated from college and has gotten married—welcome to the family Mat Cain! Jenah has graduated and is in college. Naomi and Anne are both in high school, thriving and vying for car keys. We are currently fostering Ethan, a bright and wonderful 13-year-old. The plan is to adopt him as soon as possible. It took about 23 years but I finally got my son Nathan a little brother! Big thanks to Ethan and the all the girls for talking up the books and giving copies to their teachers and others they meet. I don't know if anyone would know I was an author if it wasn't for all the support of my family!

Last but not least I want to thank Susan Stuck for helping me so much with editing and inspiring parts of this story. I honestly could not have finished this book without Susan. I also am thankful for my publisher, Nicole Smith and the great team at Faith Books & More. Thank you all so much!

TABLE OF CONTENTS

Family History and Updates...1

Chapter 1: From Ben's Journal..5

Chapter 2: Bless the Broken Road..13

Chapter 3: House of a Thousand Dreams..............................31

Chapter 4: Small Town...45

Chapter 5: I Didn't Know It at the Time................................59

Chapter 6: From Ricky's Journal..71

Chapter 7: Get Off My Back..77

Chapter 8: Better Than a Hallelujah..95

Chapter 9: Only Human..107

Chapter 10: Two Lanes of Freedom......................................113

Chapter 11: From Ben's Journal..133

Chapter 12: Boys of Fall..137

Chapter 13: From Ricky's Journal...147

Chapter 14: Heart to Heart...149

Chapter 15: From Ben's Journal..171

TABLE OF CONTENTS

Chapter 16: Fear is Easy: Love Is Hard..........................173

Chapter 17: Good Fight..185

Chapter 18: Must Be Doing Something Right................195

Chapter 19: If I Died Today..207

Chapter 20: If We Ever Needed You.............................215

Chapter 21: I Won't Let Go..221

Chapter 22: Highway Don't Care..................................227

Chapter 23: From Ricky's Journal.................................237

Chapter 24: Cry, Cry (Till the Sun Shines)....................243

Chapter 25: He Didn't Have to Be.................................259

Chapter 26: From Ricky's Journal.................................265

Chapter 27: Praying for Daylight..................................271

Chapter 28: Heart Like a Sad Song................................289

Chapter 29: If I Didn't Have You...................................295

Chapter 30: Even If It Breaks Your Heart.....................309

FAMILY HISTORY AND UPDATES

Troy James Keyton (TJ): Born in Holly Springs, Mississippi. Raised with his sister, Julie, by his mother and several abusive stepfathers. He met his biological father in his teens. Troy became a well-known country singer and had over twenty hit albums throughout his years as a country star. **Troy and Kristina** were married for sixteen years and had three children. Kristina helped Troy manage his music career and together they were raising: **Hope Marie, Gracie Sue & Mary Jane.**

Kristina died in an automobile accident because of a drunk driver. Troy raised the girls alone for five years before he met Rachel Allen.

Rachel was adopted in Oregon when she was six years old. Her biological parents are unknown. Her adoptive parents were James and Karen Smith. Rachel went to school in Colorado and married Mark Allen. They were married for ten years and had three daughters. Mark left Rachel, remarried and gave up his parental rights. Rachel raised **Bethany Lynn, Naomi Lynn & Emily Lynn** on her own for seven years.

Troy and Rachel Keyton married November 26. They blended their families and then adopted two little boys from foster care. **Benjamin James** and **Rick Allen** were five &

six at the time of the adoption and currently are thirteen and fourteen.

Beth is a school counselor working in an inner city school in Nashville. She connects families with the services offered by Hope Enterprises. She is not married. She is passionate about her work with kids. She and Rachel are talking about starting a home and school for kids that would include therapeutic interventions such as equine and art therapy.

Hope is a graphic designer with a business management degree from Belmont. She is currently the website content manager/editor for several country music stars. She also manages Katrina Metcafe's website. She married **Steve**, a youth pastor and music teacher. They met at Belmont University. They have three daughters **Amy (4), Kristina (2) and Laura (1)**. They live in Nashville and are frequent visitors at the Keyton house.

Gracie married **Danny** when they were 18. Danny has a career in the military. They currently live in West Virginia near Langley Air Force Base. He is establishing himself as an intelligence officer. His current position is as logistics planner. They have **Krissy Sue (7) and Adam (4)**.

Naomi moved back to Payton, Colorado, to take over the Hope Center that Rachel started years ago. She is the executive director of the local organization and helps to run various activities for the community. She is married to **Eric,** a young veterinarian whom she met while in Colorado. They have twin boys who are three. **Taylor and Troy.**

Emily has a business degree from Belmont. Her passion is to be a top country music artist. She has been developing her career for the several years. She is becoming well-known but also getting more caught up in the fame and lifestyle of a rising star.

Mary went to Ole Miss like her dad and sister Beth. But after taking her general education courses she wasn't sure what she wanted to do. She took a year to travel with some friends through Europe and then came back home. She is still at home and works for TJ at Hope Enterprises. She is thinking about traveling with Emily.

CHAPTER 1
From Ben's Journal

Hey, it's me, Ben Keyton. I am supposed to write about myself today. But, honestly, there isn't much to know about me, just the normal everyday stuff I guess. I am fourteen and I go to school, I play football, basketball and baseball. I really like sports, but my favorite is football. I have six older sisters. Yeah, that's right—six—and one younger brother.

I am actually supposed to tell you I was adopted when I was six. My brother Ricky and I both were adopted. It seems weird saying it or writing it. A few years ago Mama told my brother and me to write in a journal about our lives, about adoption and stuff like that. I found out I actually like writing. At least I like it more than talking so here goes.

Either way, I don't talk about adoption much—like never. I really don't like people to talk to me about it either because it just seems like a weird thing to talk about. "Hi, I'm Ben and I am adopted." See? A real conversation stopper. Just doesn't help with fitting in.

I used to worry about getting sent away, like when we first came to live here. We had a lot of different homes when we were little. But after a while, like once we started school, it just started being more normal to live here. I mean, I still had my doubts, like when I would get in trouble, and I would be really scared I might have to leave. Maybe I was fighting, destroying things, to see if they would send me away. I don't know. That's a theory some people have.

I just remember being so angry, and so scared at the same time. I was scared no one could handle me or put up with me but at the same time I just wanted to make everyone around me feel as angry as I did. Sounds crazy, and I guess it was. My parents would hold me when I raged. They told me over and over, "We got you, Ben. You are safe." It took a long time, but after a while I would relax. My mom says I had to learn how to be a kid and let them be in charge.

Now though, I really don't think about it that much. I pretty much know they are going to keep me. I've lived here longer than I did in foster care or with my birth mom. I don't want to live anywhere else, but I don't think this family would ever make us leave. I mean, we have been through some bad stuff, me and them. Okay, I put them through a lot. And they never said anything about us leaving.

I am not sure when I started believing this was my real family and that Mama and Dad were the real deal. I think it took time for me to figure it out. Sometimes I still wonder about my other mother and if she misses us, what she would

Chapter 1: From Ben's Journal

say about how good I am doing. I try not to think too much about her. I mean, she wasn't ever a real mother. I hated her for a while. Well, maybe sometimes I still do. She sure made my life harder. But I think the best thing she did was give up trying to be our mother. She pretty much sucked at it. If I think about it too much, I get really mad again.

I have never been very good talking about what is going on inside of me. I want to sometimes, but it doesn't come easy for me. I really don't know how talking about the past or about feelings helps. For a while it seemed like everyone wanted me to talk about how I felt about adoption, about my new family, about the stuff my other mother did, and how it hurt me. I didn't think it hurt me, but my parents showed me that I was acting really tough because I was afraid of getting hurt.

For a long time I didn't believe what happened to me and Ricky had anything to do with how I was acting. But I kind of think they were right. It's easier to say I am mad than to say I am hurt. It's kind of weird that I had to learn to say I was hurt or scared. But I did, because before I could see that it was like I only had an on-and-off switch for one emotion. My anger would flip on and then off, but I couldn't feel anything else. Maybe I was scared of the good feelings, too. So being happy wasn't really an option. I don't know. If I think about it too much I get confused.

I do know I am doing a lot better with stuff in general. I think being adopted and not having to worry about if my family loves me or not helps. But still, there's stuff inside me I can't let go of. I know deep down it isn't so much about adoption, it's just this gut feeling that people aren't going to like me or want me around—not at home, but like at school, on my teams, and even with my friends.

I want to belong, but I don't always feel like I do. It really sucks, too, because I do stuff I know makes people mad at me, like fighting or saying stuff I know will get me in trouble. The bad thing is, I know it will make other people tell me to leave, or kick me off their teams and still there is this thing in me that is just angry and pushes the limits. I hate myself for doing it even while I'm doing it!

Mama says it's something she struggled with, too. She says it does have to do with being adopted. She says it's like there is still this little kid in me who was abandoned and is still bruised and doesn't want to get hurt anymore. She says even wanting to belong can push on the bruise and makes it hurt, so sometimes we push people away so they stay away from the bruise. It makes sense to me when she explains it. I know I push people away unless I really trust them. Mama says the more I know the little kid in me is okay, the less protective I will feel and the less I will push people away. She also says God will help me, but I'm not so sure.

Chapter 1: From Ben's Journal

Anyway, she explains stuff pretty good and so does Ricky actually. My brother, he can talk about everything. He says what I can't and I can really talk to him. What I mean is, he says what I think or feel sometimes with words I can't seem to find. But then again, I think I get mad enough for both of us. It has always been that way. He probably wishes I would calm down and sometimes I wish he would shut up. But I'm glad he doesn't get into fights like I do, because honestly, I don't think I could handle that. Besides, I am working on using my words (Ugh, how many times my parents and my counselor have told me to use my words!), and I guess it is going better.

My dad, he told me when he was younger he got mad like I do, and he had to learn to handle stuff a better way. He told me once he was mad about things that happened to him and his sister when they were little kids. He said his grandpa—I never met him—but he helped him trust in God. And Dad said when he was growing up God helped him learn to put his energy into sports. I want to try to do that because it worked for Dad. But I think my dad was better at getting along with his teams than I am. I get along with my family, and that's about it. And even that took a long time. Dad reminds me he had to learn to trust God. Since I don't like to talk about God, we talk about sports and how to work with the team. Dad talks to me about this a lot.

"Play hard, but don't let your anger come out against your teammates," he says. "They are your brothers and they need you." *I don't know.* Sometimes when I am really frustrated, hitting a baseball or running a tackle play does help, but I get just as upset with the guys on my team as I do the other team.

I think my dad understands that sometimes I need to just hit the crap out of the punching bag in the garage. Mama is always reminding me to use my words, but Dad really gets that there are no words for the angry part of me.

Ricky says it is harder for me because I remember more of what happened to us when we were young. He thinks that's why I have such a hard time to trust and believe in people. Ricky and Mama both see the good in people no matter what. One thing though, I might really fight it, especially when I want to do what I want to do, but I do believe in my family. I know Ricky and I would die for each other, and I know my sisters really care about me, too. My parents have been through a lot of good and bad times with all of us kids and they still seem to like everyone and always show us they are there for us. Always.

I guess I am doing better though. I feel like I am. Like, I can feel when the anger is there now before it takes over. Even with Kyle, this kid on my football team who hates me,

Chapter 1: From Ben's Journal

I have been able to walk away. I never could do that before.

I feel like I have to try so much harder than other people, harder than Ricky even, just to be okay. That is really annoying because we have the same crap that happened to us. Ricky says it's not the same though because he had me to protect him, and I had no one.

I think that is one thing that has changed for sure. I don't feel like I have to fight to keep Ricky and me safe. I still mess up a lot, but I know my family is safe. I don't have to prove myself or protect myself with this family. I can make mistakes and they still are there for me, like I was for Ricky. Sometimes maybe I am still testing this out, but it's getting me deep down inside, maybe even deeper than the anger.

I realized something a little while ago: I don't feel so scared. I feel comfortable with my family. And that is saying a lot, because most of the time I feel uncomfortable even with myself and figuring out who I am.

CHAPTER 2
Bless the Broken Road

"Atta boy!" Rachel heard TJ's deep voice across the school yard as she and her younger son, Ricky, made their way over to the high school football field. Her husband and older son, Ben, were entrenched in a long tough practice. It was the final workout before the team's first game of the season.

Though not officially the coach, TJ had been helping with Heritage High's sporting programs since their daughters had been students. Rachel shielded her eyes from the late afternoon sun as it slipped toward the Tennessee mountains, the summer heat giving way to the cool of evening.

She couldn't see him yet, but she could picture his six-foot-one frame hunkered down, his Tennessee Titan's hat pulled low to shield his dark brown eyes. He would be pacing the sidelines clapping his hands and shouting encouragement to the team. TJ was every bit as intense a coach as he had been performing on stage for thousands of country music fans.

The first time Rachel had ever seen him was in Colorado when she and her friend Jenna were part of a sold-out crowd. That was long before she knew him as TJ. Her encounters with him then were through his music. She and the world knew him as Troy Keyton, a household name for Rachel, her girls, and of course, thousands of others. His voice and charisma had earned him twenty years of big hits and top-selling albums. Back then Rachel never dreamed of really knowing him. For that she had to thank her own notoriety as a small-time community leader and counselor.

As she approached the on-going practice, Rachel saw TJ run out to the field and offer instructions to a couple of the young men. She gave a little laugh. She was amazed that at age fifty-six he still lived with such intensity. He might have retired from his persona as Troy Keyton country star, but his zest for life had not waned at all. She hoped she could continue to keep up with him because he didn't show any intention of growing old or slowing down.

Rachel and TJ had each brought three teen or pre-teen daughters to their blended family. Rachel's ex-husband had left his family for a new life when Emily, their youngest, had been only five years old. Rachel had been raising her daughters alone for seven years when she met TJ whose wife had been tragically killed by a drunk driver three years earlier.

Everything had happened so quickly. Rachel had moved to Tennessee and married TJ within a year of their first date. A short time later, TJ had decided to completely retire from the

Chapter 2: Bless the Broken Road

music scene. Before long, he joined and continued to develop programs for abused children Rachel had established. While Rachel worked with parents and children with difficulties, TJ found his niche helping boys growing up without fathers.

Rachel and TJ had been married three years when two boys needing a permanent home, six-year-old Ben and five-year-old Ricky, had come to live with them. Rachel was no stranger to kids with a load of past trauma and pain. Not only was she a family therapist specializing in abused children, she had worked for years with a camp specifically for foster children.

Seven years ago Ben and Ricky's adoptions were finalized. TJ and Rachel's daughters had all—each in her own way—embraced their little brothers. Though the girls were now either headed to college or living on their own, Rachel realized the boys had lived with their family longer than they had lived anywhere else.

Rachel stood near the sideline watching Ben scrimmage with the team. At fourteen, he seemed to be growing bigger and taller every day. He looked so much like TJ no one ever questioned whose son he was. They shared the same dark brown hair, deep brown eyes and similar facial features, including dimples that appeared when they smiled.

From stories she had heard, Ben wasn't much different in

temperament from TJ as a young man either. They both loved football, baseball and girls; pretty much in that order. They were both extremely competitive, often angry and always intense. TJ confessed to Rachel more than once that he and Ben were so much alike it scared him straight to his knees. Rachel knew they were both headstrong and stubborn. TJ had overcome his own troubled childhood in the same way they hoped Ben would.

Ricky was thirteen and in eighth grade. He and Ben looked like siblings around their eyes, but they were different in many ways. Though slighter in build, Rick recently had grown tall and lanky. His face was thinner than TJ's and Ben's, but he sported dimples similar to theirs. Light brown hair set off Rick's blue eyes, far less somber than his older brother's.

Ricky had a great sense of humor, but was also very sensitive and at times more emotional. Where Ben was slow to trust people, Rick loved everyone immediately. Everyone was a friend, even someone he had just met. Ricky was easy going and fairly good-natured. From the start he had embraced his family and seemed happy to have a lot of people and a lot of activity around him.

Both boys had attended a public elementary school. The goal had been to switch them over to Heritage Christian Academy for middle school, but it had taken a few years for them to get caught up academically and ready for the change. Heritage had a high academic standard and an excellent sporting program. It was the school TJ's kids had attended and where Rachel's also graduated once they moved from Colorado. Heritage was a tough school where more was demanded in terms of school work and performance.

Rachel watched Ben run down the field. He was such an athletic kid, strong, intelligent and good looking though difficult for others to connect with. He fought daily to control his temper and didn't make friends easily. He had the potential to be a star athlete, but being part of a team was not easy for him. It took everyone working together to encourage him. The need to belong and the tendency to push people away were opposing forces fighting for control in him making him hard for people to understand. Would Heritage give him the leeway to figure it out?

Ben was one tough cookie. He could be charming and once you got to know him, he was loyal. If you made it through his tough exterior, he would be your friend for life. He just didn't let a lot of people in. Between Rick and Ben, it was Ben who was actually the deep thinker and more serious about life. He was content to have a few people in his life he considered trustworthy. He didn't need companionship or approval like Rick did.

A small crowd of parents were gathered, watching the

final minutes of practice. One of them complimented Rachel on how Ben was doing. She thanked him. In Tennessee, especially in their little town, high school sports were community events. Several of the mothers and fathers that watched every practice and game were community leaders, clergymen, even the local sheriff.

They were attentive, and way too fanatical for Rachel's taste. Take, for example, Lisa Wright who was near the goal line. Every sport Lisa was there hooting and hollering for someone to pass the ball to her son. There were six Wright boys who played sports for Heritage. Rachel had seen Lisa yell at refs and argue with coaches. Last year during a basketball game she had actually called the coach on his cell phone to tell him what play she thought should be run. It had become a family joke.

Rachel loved football—all sports—especially watching her kids play; she was athletic and competitive. But no, she did not put herself in the same category as some of the other parents. When things became too intense Rachel tended to just walk away. Now, watching TJ as he shouted to the offensive line, she was glad he wasn't one of those hellish parents. As a coach he was good at channeling his energy into encouragement.

Rachel glanced at Rick standing next to her. He had grown up playing flag football with Ben and TJ. He just never loved it the way Ben did. He chewed on his fingernail

Chapter 2: Bless the Broken Road

as he watched his dad and brother.

Running was more Rick's passion, and recently, tennis. He definitely liked the less aggressive sports. He ran cross country in the fall and played tennis in the spring. He was competitive in his own way, preferring to challenge himself more than competing with others.

As soon as Rachel saw the offensive team line up she felt the tension. She had noticed Ben roughly bump another boy as they took their places. It was Kyle Evens, the kid Ben had complained about all summer. They were both running backs. Kyle, a sophomore, had been in line to hold the starting position until Ben showed up for summer tryouts. It was well-known and often talked about among the coaching staff and die-hard sideline fans that Ben was bigger, faster and probably better than the older boy. What Ben lacked was experience. Unfortunately, he was gaining a reputation as one who was quick to fight.

TJ knew Kyle was threatened by Ben's raw natural ability. While the coaches focused with both young men on working together and becoming solid in their skills, the two simply did not like each other. Being part of the squad and working hard without getting himself thrown out of a game or off the team was going to be a challenge and the real victory for Ben throughout the season. If Kyle and Ben could work together they would be a dynamic duo for the offense.

"Hell," TJ had said just last night, "if Ben could work with anyone as part of a team it would be amazing."

The stakes were higher for Ben this year. Moving from junior high football to the high school varsity was a huge step up. Rachel worried, knowing switching to Heritage and their competitive programs might prove to be more than Ben could handle. Even with a full summer practice schedule and time to get adjusted, she was apprehensive about overloading Ben. Would it prove to be too much stress?

Part of why TJ was coaching was to stay close by Ben. But even so, the pressures of increased academic standards and needing to perform on the field were a lot for a child with Ben's background. Rachel did what she could to keep things steady and calm at home. Through their steadfast support and structure in their home environment, she and TJ had seen both boys grow and heal. She kept her fingers crossed, knowing change was challenging for her sons.

Today Kyle was playing tight end and blocking for Ben who was running back. She watched nervously, keyed into the mood shifts she saw often in her older son. Rick, standing next to her, saw it, too. "Uh-oh," he uttered under his breath. "Ben's pissed."

Rachel gave Rick a nervous look and they both laughed when they crossed their fingers at the same time for good

Chapter 2: Bless the Broken Road

luck. Rick was just about eye level with her five-foot-six. A couple more inches and he would pass her. Most people thought Rick favored Rachel's facial features and thinner athletic build though Rick had expressive blue eyes while hers were green, and Rick's light brown hair often appeared darker than Rachel's, matted with sweat from cross country running. They were most similar in the way they responded empathically to the world around them. If she was nervous about the tension on the field it was no surprise Rick also sensed it. Watching his brother, he bit his lip.

She and Ricky were usually the first to pick up on Ben's triggers and when he was escalating. They stood together, tense, watching the drama unfold. Rachel drew a deep breath and said a silent prayer. Rachel herself had been adopted at six years of age and, like Rick, her older brother had had an explosive temperament.

Ben took the hand-off from the quarterback and started up the right side of the field. He made it past the player blocked by the left tackle, but then hit a wall when the outside linebacker smashed into him, taking him down hard. Ben jumped quickly to his feet, mad as a hornet. The collision must have hurt because anger was his customary response to pain. He threw off his helmet, yelling and swearing. He marched over to Kyle who was supposed to have blocked Bryce, the senior linebacker.

Rachel wanted to look away or run out on the field to stop what was coming. Instead a sinking feeling glued her to her spot on the sideline. Come on Ben, she silently soothed. Don't do it. She held her breath. Rick was shaking his head, also silently willing his brother to walk away.

Ben stood nose to nose with Kyle and grabbed the front of his shirt. His words carried to all the parents standing by. TJ and the other coaches sprinted toward the boys. Reluctantly, Ben turned his body away though his posture remained aggressive and challenging. "Damn it Evens! You're supposed to keep him off me." He added a few more curses despite the school policy against foul language.

Kyle took off his helmet and met Ben's glare. "Who the hell do you think you are, Keyton? Router is the best linebacker in the freakin' league and twice my size. You just can't take a hit. Plus you're pissed because you know Coach is starting me tomorrow. Stupid-ass freshman." He pushed Ben away from him. "Back off, Keyton!"

Ben raised his fist. Rachel knew if he hit his teammate he would likely not only sit out tomorrow's game but most of the season. With his background, she didn't know if he would get another chance. She could barely breathe. How many games had she watched the past couple years that ended with Ben in the middle of a fight?

Chapter 2: Bless the Broken Road

TJ stepped closer to the young men. He didn't say a word, but even from where she stood, his presence was influential. TJ was far enough away to give Ben the benefit of the doubt but close enough to stop him if he decided to throw a punch. Ben returned Kyle's glare with a stony silence that Rachel was sure every player and parent could feel. Ben's hands were in tight fists and both kids held expressions of anger. The tension was so thick it seemed to hang in the air.

"Go ahead, hit me," Kyle taunted. "You think you're such a big shot."

TJ moved a step closer to Kyle.

"I'm not afraid to hit you, Evens." Ben looked like he was going to spit in Kyle's face. He glanced at his dad and swallowed hard. Rachel noticed his fingers relax, unclenching his fists. He was doing his best to gain control of himself. Ben looked Kyle in the eye again. "I ain't gonna give you the satisfaction of seeing me get in trouble." He moved past Kyle with a strong bump to the shoulder. "Just do your damn job and keep that ape off me next time." He picked up his helmet, not giving Kyle another word.

Kyle turned and stared after him with distain. For a moment it looked as if Kyle might continue the argument, but then he turned toward his teammates and made a boorish comment about Ben being on the team because of TJ and how pitiful it was when freshmen tried to play varsity.

"Hey," Coach Fischer hollered and then blew his whistle for the team to huddle up.

Rachel couldn't hear all the coach was saying, but she could tell from the groans it wasn't what the players wanted to hear. Coach Fischer had a reputation for bringing teams together, honing raw talent and upholding the school's mission to train students to be respectful and responsible. He enforced strict rules for his athletes and Rachel guessed at least part of the chewing-out would include the boys' attitudes and foul language.

As the team huddled, TJ jogged over to Rachel and Rick. The exchange between Ben and Kyle hadn't seemed to dampen his spirits at all. He ruffled Rick's hair playfully and leaned in to give Rachel a peck on the lips. His grin was contagious and she smiled warmly at him. She loved how he greeted her as though he hadn't seen her every day for the last twelve years. He could still make her heart skip a beat with a hello kiss.

"We're just about done," he told her, "except for the extra laps they have to run thanks to Ben and Kyle." He greeted a couple of the parents nearby then whispered in Rachel's ear, "Did you see Ben back down? That was pretty amazing for our son, don't you think?"

Chapter 2: Bless the Broken Road

Rachel agreed. They had been encouraging these small steps of progress for the past seven years. Now it was practically habit for them to bring out the positive aspects even when something didn't go as well as they hoped. It was one way they helped each other keep moving forward rather than getting stuck in a negative pattern. Unfortunately, not everyone could see how far Ben had come; they had to deal with the behaviors they could see.

"Hey Dad, can I jog with them?" Ricky asked, already starting off. TJ waved him the go-ahead. They watched Ricky sprint to catch the older boys. He met them halfway across the field and elbowed Ben in a brotherly fashion. Together they finished the second half of the track.

While Ben and Kyle started their extra drills the other kids took off for the showers. Ricky dropped down and did the sit-ups and push-ups alongside his brother. When they finished, Kyle quickly jumped to his feet and offered Ricky a hand up. Ben scowled. Rick refused the gesture and got up on his own, standing solidly beside his brother. Kyle gave Rick a cold, hard stare.

Rachel noticed Ben's fists clench again. She was about to draw TJ's attention to what looked like another conflict when Kyle turned angrily and headed off toward the showers. She let out a sigh of relief. She and TJ followed the boys in the direction of the parking lot beyond the gym. Ben opened the locker room door.

"Dude, make it fast 'cause I'm starvin'!" Rick called, an affectionate grin on his face, and rushed to catch up with Rachel and TJ.

Rachel couldn't help but laugh as TJ pulled Ricky into a headlock while they bantered about who was still the fastest. The kid never seemed to run out of energy. He ran everywhere. She listened contently while Rick filled in his dad on his cross-country practice and the big meet coming up Saturday morning. As they approached the vehicles they were suddenly interrupted by one of the football players rushing out of the gym.

"Coach Keyton!" the half-clad teen yelled. "We need you!"

Rachel's stomach knotted as TJ took off after the boy. Ricky started to follow, but Rachel put her hand on his arm.

"Let Dad go, Rick." Whenever Ben was in trouble Rick instinctively wanted to be closer to him. It wasn't to protect him. Ricky wasn't one to fight. But maybe it was to protect Ben from himself. From the time they were little boys, if Ben was upset Rick would be next to him as if they were joined at the hip. Rachel had seen Rick comfort his brother through countless bad dreams and even worse moods. She hoped whatever was going on in the locker room didn't involve

Chapter 2: Bless the Broken Road

Ben, but like Rick, she instinctively knew it was probably all about Ben.

She and Rick stood at the cars, waiting anxiously, side by side. Finally, TJ came out with Ben, still in his practice uniform, following begrudgingly behind. They both looked disgruntled. It was clear TJ was angry and Ben was sullen. Rachel squared her shoulders. It wasn't the first time she had seen this scene.

Ben moved past her without a word. He roughly tossed his backpack, football helmet, cleats and shoulder pads into the back of her SUV. Then he silently yet purposefully got in the passenger side and slammed the door. Rachel questioned TJ with her eyes. He shrugged, exasperated. "Guess he is going with you."

"What happened?" Rachel asked, then quickly added, "Do I want to know?"

"Same old stuff. You know. Probably just couldn't let it go with Kyle. When I got in there the both of them were on the floor exchanging blows. Kyle was on top of Ben swinging away while the other kids stood around watching and hollering. Coach Fischer had gone to another part of the gym, but he got in there about the same time I did. I pulled 'em apart and held onto Ben while Coach Fischer kept Kyle away from him." TJ shook his head. "Dang. We almost got through all of preseason without a single actual fight." His face was a mixture of disbelief and disappointment. "Coach is pretty mad. He told the boys to get out of his locker room. He'll deal with them later, I suppose."

Rachel, full of empathy, touched his arm softly. She shrugged and said as lighthearted as she could, "Three steps forward, two steps back is still progress, right?" He nodded but he didn't look too encouraged.

Rachel glanced over at Ricky still waiting beside her. "Well, shoot." There wasn't much she could do to help right now. "Let's get home and eat dinner." Turning to her younger son, she said, "Hey, Ricky, why don't you ride with Dad since Ben is already in my car." Not long ago Ben would have chosen to be with just about anyone except her. Rick was a good antidote for TJ in same way he often calmed Ben down.

Rachel got in the driver's seat and looked over at Ben. He had changed his shoes and was out of his pads, but his practice clothes were dirty, his face smeared with grime and sweat. It looked like the left side of his face was starting to swell. Rachel wrinkled her nose. With Ben's gear in the back, his dirty uniform and lack of a shower, the smell of sweat, dirt and football was overpowering. Rachel turned the car on and hit the window down button.

Chapter 2: Bless the Broken Road

Ben didn't look at her. He sat sullenly with his head down. Rachel studied him for a second. His hands and feet were already much bigger than hers. But when he had such a disturbed scowl all she saw was the hurt little boy in him. It was his "I'm-probably-in-trouble-but-I'm-trying-not-to-care" look. Her heart filled with compassion for his struggle. For all his pain and anger, Rachel admired his tenacity.

"Buckle up," she reminded him gently.

He stole a glance at her as he stretched the seatbelt around until it clicked. She didn't look away, appraising his face. "Looks like you are going to have a shiner." She pointed to his cheek. "Let's get home and put something on that." She put the vehicle in gear and followed TJ's yellow jeep out of the parking lot.

Ben didn't respond, but she could see his shoulders relax just a bit. She had learned over the years that it did no good to chastise a kid in the moment when they were already beat down. She figured Ben probably knew he had blown it. He certainly looked discouraged. Rachel was sure whatever consequences the coach handed out were going to impact him far more than anything she could say. She found herself wishing again that he didn't have to fight so hard. Exhaling heavily, she silently breathed a simple prayer for her son as they rode home without speaking.

CHAPTER 3
House of a Thousand Dreams

Rachel enlisted Rick's help setting the table for dinner. It was apparent he was hanging around to talk with her while Ben was upstairs showering. Just as obvious was the fact that Ricky needed a shower, too. When he reached above his head to get glasses out of the cupboard Rachel could smell him from across the kitchen.

"Ew! She wrinkled her nose in disgust. "Ricky, you smell like moldy old gym socks!"

"I can't shower right now. I'm starving, Mama, and I can't even think of anything else."

They bantered back and forth. She chided him about whether he thought the meal might be ruined for everyone else. He laughed easily and pretended he had no idea what she was talking about. "I'm just trying to help you," he insisted. "Besides Ben's up there now and he needs it way more than me." Rachel was quick to remind him there were plenty more showers in the huge house.

The boys had taken over the entire second floor as the girls had left home one after another. There were five bedrooms and three full baths upstairs. Once upon a time the entire level had been filled with "girly stuff" as Rick called it. However, a few years earlier Rachel had redecorated the upper floor to suit the boys. Ben and Ricky each had a room and Rachel decorated the extra rooms for her grandsons. Where once there had been a girls' playroom with toys, stuffed animals and tea parties, now there was a large game room complete with the latest X-Box video madness.

That was against Rachel's better judgment as she was well aware of the adverse effects of video games, especially on kids with trauma histories. She had only agreed to it as long as TJ enforced strict guidelines. It was important for the boys to have limited time to isolate themselves. They also restricted amounts of screen time. TJ arranged the room to be used only with permission and most of the time he kept it locked. Otherwise, all the kids would spend hours in the game room. Even the grandkids had to earn time to play video games.

The basement contained a full gym and a recording/music studio. It had always been considered "the man cave" where TJ had his office, his musical equipment, and a pool table among other things. The girls were not prohibited, of course, and through the years it had become a hangout when they had bigger family gatherings. If the men—TJ and the sons-in-law—were not outside, they could usually be found

Chapter 3: *House of a Thousand Dreams*

downstairs shooting pool or in an impromptu jam session.

On the main level Rachel had set up the boys' old rooms for the younger grandchildren. They had installed a door between the rooms so they could be one giant playroom, or if desired, two separate rooms. Two additional rooms were decorated for the granddaughters. TJ had worried the house would be too big after all the children grew up and moved out, but with the constant flow of visiting grandchildren, the addition of the boys, and their daughters and friends staying over now and then, it rarely seemed empty.

The oldest of the girls, Beth, thirty years old, lived nearby in Nashville. She worked as a school counselor and opened her own private practice as a licensed therapist. She loved working with families and children with challenges. Neither she nor her younger sisters, Emily and Mary, were married or had their own children.

Perhaps because she was Rachel's oldest, Rachel and Beth shared a unique bond. They also shared similarities in their careers and ideas. Beth was a solid lover of God and seemed content where He had her in life. She had no plans to marry or have children, claiming that in the ones she served, she already had hundreds.

Hope, TJ's oldest daughter, was also in Nashville. She worked from home as a website content manager for several country music stars. Hope was incredibly busy raising her three daughters, four-year-old Amy, two-year-old Kristina, and the newest, eight-month-old baby Laura. Her husband, Steve, was a youth pastor and music teacher. Of all his girls, Hope looked the most like her dad, but according to TJ, she was more like her mother in how solid a person she turned out to be.

Rachel was continually amazed at the passion with which she and Steve pursued God in raising their family. Hope had always been Daddy's girl and it meant the world to her that Steve was a man her daddy loved and respected. Their family was often around on Sunday afternoons, giving Rachel and TJ lots of grandparent time with their little girls.

Gracie and Danny had married their first year out of high school. Gracie was eighteen and pregnant. Their choices had forced them to grow up and make decisions beyond their years. But they had weathered those early storms. Danny was currently in the Air Force working on the Langley Base in West Virginia. As a young teen, he had been mentored by TJ through the programs for boys without dads.

TJ had been so disappointed when Gracie and Danny had come to them with the news about the baby. But looking back, Rachel saw God's hand in all of it. Of all TJ's children, Gracie had outwardly struggled most with her mother, Kris's death. She had been mad at God for years and had a hard

Chapter 3: *House of a Thousand Dreams*

time accepting Rachel as part of the family. During her pregnancy, as she tried to decide whether to give the baby up for adoption, Gracie had given her life to God. All that had brought Gracie and Rachel closer.

Now Krissy Sue was seven, the oldest of the grandchildren. She looked a great deal like her namesake, her maternal grandmother, Gracie. Krissy and four-year-old Adam came to the farm often, especially summer and holidays. Danny worked long hours on and off the base, but he visited as often as he could.

Five years ago, Naomi had moved away from the farm to her hometown of Peyton, Colorado as director of the Hope Center, an organization Rachel had founded years before meeting TJ. When the opportunity opened for Naomi to go to Peyton, it had been met with mixed feelings. Naomi was excellent with horses, and she and Rachel had been working together providing equine-assisted therapy. Rachel didn't want her to leave. Like Beth, Naomi had an ease with children.

The move turned out to be the best thing for Naomi. She was in Peyton less than a year when she met the local veterinarian. According to Naomi, it was love at first sight, at least for her. But it didn't take long for Dr. Eric to ask her to marry him. After four years of marriage and a set of two-year-old twin boys, Naomi continued to manage the Hope

Center while Eric ran his practice. Next summer Troy and Taylor would be old enough to stay at the farm with Papa and G-ma for a week.

Emily, Rachel's youngest, was usually on the road. Her music career was beginning to take off. TJ had gotten her started with some great connections. Their good friend Katrina Metcafe and TJ pulled as many strings as they could without interfering too much. Emily was strong-willed and stubborn with a real desire to make a name for herself. TJ taught her that no matter how much they helped her, in the end it would be up to Emily herself how far she went.

It worried Rachel how much Emily's career was changing her. Through high school, Emily had been part of their church's worship team. She had wanted to get going with her music right after graduation, but TJ and Rachel insisted she at least get some college under her belt. They had hoped that would buy some time to increase her maturity before she jumped into the music scene. Emily surprised them by completing her business degree at Belmont then going right from playing at church to playing in bars. As soon as TJ could arrange it, she started touring with more well-known artists.

At first she was the opening act for the opening band. But after her first year on the road she had gotten a recording deal and was already working on a second album. Rachel was certain her latest song, a catchy country number, was

Chapter 3: House of a Thousand Dreams

headed straight for the top of the charts.

Emily heavy on her mind, Rachel changed the rice from the cooker to a bowl and set it on the table. Emily was due in town this weekend. It had been a while since the family had seen her and she had no plans to settle down. Rachel was hopeful she would come Friday night to see her brother play in his first high school football game. TJ had warned Rachel Emily's transient lifestyle was just getting started.

Rachel was just finishing with a salad when Mary, the youngest of their daughters, slipped into the kitchen through the patio door. Mary lived in the little cottage behind the house. Danny and Gracie had fixed it up and lived there when they were first married. It had been occupied ever since. After Gracie and Danny moved into military housing TJ's sister, Julie, and her son had lived there for six months after TJ's dad had died. Then Rachel's long-time friend, Jenna, had needed a place to live for a short time when she returned from the mission field. After Jenna got married, Mary had taken over the cottage.

Of all the girls, Mary was the least structured and the least certain what she really wanted to do with her life. She was a great assistant for TJ and his various projects. She also helped Rachel with the business end of the equine therapy. She had a business administration degree from Ole Miss, where her dad and Beth had gone to school. Mary was in no hurry to get out on her own. Rachel was sure the ease of living independently in the cottage while having the benefit of family added to Mary's "failure to launch." But truth be told, Rachel and TJ enjoyed having her close by. She was a huge asset for both of them. Mary was happy-go-lucky and loved life and family.

"Hey, little bro," Mary said playfully to Rick as she tousled his hair. He darted away but returned her greeting with a big grin. "How was practice? Let me guess; you ran 150 miles, didn't you?" Mary loved to tease Ricky about running since for herself, she hated the very idea of it.

"Yeah, Mare, I ran 150 miles—per hour that is."

Rachel shook her head and smiled at the exchange between them. She was getting the meat out of the oven just as Ben came into the kitchen.

"I'm starving," he said to no one in particular. "Is it ready?"

"Soon as your daddy gets in here." She had to dart out of the way to keep him from grabbing a piece of food as she went by with the plate of meat.

Mary yelled down to TJ's office to get him to hurry up.

"Coming!" he hollered back.

Chapter 3: House of a Thousand Dreams

The family gathered around the table. TJ joined the circle and they held hands as he prayed over their food and family.

Once seated, Mary casually asked Ben if he was going to play in the first big game of the season. She had no idea what she had just jumped into. Rachel caught TJ's eye. He bit his lip and shrugged slightly. There was a pause as they all looked with interest to Ben.

Pretending to be entranced with his food, he didn't respond. Mary gave him a nudge. He hesitated before shoveling in more food. With his mouth full, he muttered, "I don't know." Then he added sullenly, "Prob'ly not now." He took another bite then ventured a look up from his plate.

Even though he noticed the family watching him, waiting for his response, he didn't offer more information. He quickly looked down again and continued to eat.

On the way home he had said nothing to Rachel beyond, "It wasn't my fault." Rachel hadn't pushed him. Like most teens, he rarely thought it was his fault. It was getting better, but both her boys struggled to own their part of problems in their lives.

Mary looked at her dad who was looking at Ben. "Okay, you all. Am I missing something here?"

Rick gave a slight headshake and a look meant to warn

Mary to tread lightly. But she was fearless when it came to jumping into messes.

"What? Did you get in a fight again?"

Ben glared at her but didn't answer. Mary drew her own conclusions. "Yep. Now, I see it. You've got a shiner there. You were fighting. Dang it, Ben, when are you gonna learn that fighting only gets you on the bench?"

Mary looked disapproving. As her words hung over the dinner table, no one else said anything for a moment.

Rachel found it interesting how siblings could call each other out on things parents could not. Rachel herself had not grown up with a family of close brothers and sisters, so she didn't have that personal experience. As her children had gotten older, Rachel had come to value the interaction between siblings. She discovered she enjoyed the camaraderie, even though it could be tense at times. She loved it when TJ and his sister Julie joked around and teased each other. Julie could say certain things to TJ and hold him accountable in ways no one else could. Rachel ducked her chin to hide her smile, waiting for Mary to get the story from Ben. She would.

"It wasn't my fault," Ben insisted morosely. He shook his head. Then he looked sideways at TJ to see his reaction. No one responded. Ben huffed, "You always think it's me. But this time I swear, it wasn't."

Chapter 3: House of a Thousand Dreams

Again it was Mary who spoke right to the issue. "You always say it's not your fault, little bro, but somehow it's always you that ends up sitting out the game or getting sent home." She emphasized the "always" both times.

"Whatever." He shook his head again and looked down at his food. Rachel noticed TJ watching him intently. "You don't have to believe me," he muttered, picking at his food.

"Hey, wait a minute. Not 'whatever,'" TJ said with interest and concern. "I haven't heard what really happened." Ben looked up at him quickly. TJ was nonchalant, inviting Ben to speak openly. "Want to tell us?"

"It's not like you're going to believe me anyway," Ben looked away from his dad and returned to staring at his food and pushing it around his plate.

"Try me."

Ben looked up slowly at each of them in turn. Rachel noticed what TJ must have sensed. Ben didn't look angry or defiant as he usually did when hiding something. He looked hurt, and broken. Rachel nodded in agreement and told him softly that she would like to hear about it, too.

Rick nudged him with his arm. "Hey man, you never get a shiner like that in fights you start, so something must'a happened. Tell us."

Ben nodded and then bit his lip. Rachel couldn't help but feel proud of their family and the soft place it provided for all of them—a place to fail, to fall, to bounce to greater heights. She was deeply thankful for the trust and care she knew these boys had here.

"Okay. Fine. So I was plenty mad at Kyle," he admitted. "He had been on my case all through practice, but I made up my mind I wasn't going to fight him no matter what. I know for sure if I lost control, I could get kicked out of school completely, not just the team. 'No matter what,' I told myself, 'I am not gonna fight.'" He looked at his dad to see his reaction. TJ encouraged him to continue.

"I went into the locker room and Kyle was right there by my locker. He started saying all this crap about practice and telling me I was no good." Ben shook his head at the memory of it. "But I just pushed past him, told him to shut up. But he wouldn't let up. One of the other guys, a senior, even told him the same thing. That really pisse—" He glanced at Rachel and then corrected himself, "—made him mad. I was just trying to get my gear off, decided to skip getting showered so I could just get away from him before I did something. But the next thing I knew he grabbed me from behind and threw me down. He was yelling at me to hit him."

Ben took a deep breath. "But I wouldn't. All I could think of was you—" He pointed to TJ. "—telling me, one fight and

Chapter 3: House of a Thousand Dreams

you're off the team. He hit me anyway." Ben's eyes watered. "But I never hit him, Daddy. Mama. Honest. I know you thought I was hitting him too, but Dad, I was just trying to block his fists. If you see him tomorrow, he isn't going to have one bruise on his face."

Mary swore under her breath. "It's okay, little bro. Me and Ricky will go beat the crap outta him." She—with all of her slender 5'4" frame—was charged at the injustice of someone picking on her brother.

Rick tried to echo her enthusiasm, but he preferred justice be won with words. "Can't you talk to the coach, Dad? The other kids should tell him the truth, too."

"I sure will, Son." TJ said. He turned to Ben. "I am proud of you, Ben, taking those punches without fighting back. That must have been the hardest thing you have ever done."

Ben shrugged indifferently, but he looked away, embarrassed at the praise. Rachel caught a tiny lift at the corners of his mouth before he dove back into his food.

When Rachel thought about it later that night in the quiet of her room, her earlier wish that Ben would learn he didn't have to fight so hard came to mind. Maybe it was happening. That was more than a small step for Ben—it was a giant leap.

After dinner, TJ called Coach Fischer. Ben was standing nearby. TJ told the coach what Ben had said. Then he handed the phone to Ben so he could tell his side of the story to Coach Fischer. Rachel was trying to stay out of the way, but she was close enough to see and hear Ben. As with most children who struggle with attachment and anger issues, there was a deep-rooted sense of always being wrong that played into the notion that everyone was out to get him. Ben would rather be in control of accusations and bad actions than risk hoping he could come out on top of a bad situation.

Rachel knew this moment, seeing his family standing by him, believing the best in him, was very important. So many times in the past he wouldn't even try to do the right thing, feeling that deep inside he was bad anyway and certain no one ever believed in him. Trust was built over time and with a child as hurt as Ben, it took countless small but powerful moments to bring healing and hope. Tonight, with his family standing strongly beside him, Rachel could see another brick laid on the path of trust and acceptance.

Coach said he would make a few more calls. Later, when he called back, it was to let Ben know that two of his teammates had confirmed what Ben said. Kyle would be sitting out the game. Coach wanted Ben dressed and ready to play. Rachel wasn't sure if that meant Ben would start the game, but he was ecstatic just to know he could play. He and Rick danced around the kitchen with excitement. It reminded Rachel of when they were little boys. It felt good to be able to celebrate such a victory.

CHAPTER 4
Small Town

The bleachers were filling up fast. Rachel was seated and greeting parents and kids from past and present years at Heritage. The team would soon take the field. The marching band entertained the home crowd. Nothing felt quite like the strong sense of community pride on game night. Even before this year, the Keytons had spent a lot of Friday nights watching Heritage football. Of course, now that Ben would be playing, Rachel was discovering just how nerve-racking it could be waiting for the game to start.

Mary and Rick had gone to find their friends while Rachel sat holding seats for them and others. First to arrive were Hope and Steve with their girls. Rachel waved them over. In a few short moments Rachel found her arms full of wiggly excited grandchildren very happy to see their Na-Na.

Rachel's phone chimed, indicating a text message. Emily was on her way but running late. She asked Rachel to save a few seats.

Beth caught Rachel's eye with a wave and worked her way through the crowd. Before she even sat down she lifted Baby Laura from Rachel's arms, giving Kristina and Amy an opportunity to snuggle in close. Thankfully, Hope had brought a bag full of little toys and books. Hope, finding her arms free, chatted easily with her sister and snapped a picture of Rachel reading to her two- and four-year-old granddaughters.

"This is their first game and they are so excited," Hope explained. "They have been talking about seeing Ben play 'tootball' all day. Except Kristina has been getting really mad at Amy saying it's not 'tootball' it's 'sootball.' I suspect this is going to be a short night for us though." Hope handed Rachel another cardboard storybook.

Steve added, "Yeah, I'm not sure how long we will be able to keep them entertained once they realize Uncle Ben won't be playing any kind of ball with them. But at least we made it."

Rachel nodded understanding. She knew how difficult it could be attending these sorts of events with three small children. She thanked Steve for bringing everyone for Ben's game then began *The Runaway Bunny* for a second time. Beth and Hope continued chatting, catching up on each other's lives.

Rachel had just finished another story about three cute little kittens learning to listen and obey when she spotted Mike and Tina Metcafe, her dearest friends. Beth handed the

Chapter 4: Small Town

baby to Hope and coaxed her nieces to move over to make some room near Rachel. Rachel was so happy to see her friends, she stood and waved, urging them to come quickly.

Tina led the way up the bleachers. Mike, who had just celebrated his sixty-fifth birthday, cracked jokes about being much too old to climb that high. He loved to complain to Rachel about the hassles her kids caused him, but truth was, he never missed a game when their kids were involved. Rachel laughed and harassed him back about being old and cranky. She told him to pipe down and save his voice for cheering.

Tina was a small, slender woman, but fun-loving and known for her spunk. Mike frequently teased her about being short and sassy. Rachel loved her wit and southern charm. She was outspoken and genuine. When she had met Tina it was like finding a sister. They were both fifty-seven with birthdays just a week apart.

Long before Rachel met TJ, he and Mike had been like brothers. The Metcafes and the Keytons were best friends, and they had welcomed Rachel with open hearts. It had been Tina's idea to introduce Rachel to TJ. Tina was, in fact, the reason Rachel had come to Tennessee in the first place.

Back then Rachel Allen had been a small-town single mother in Colorado running a non-profit organization. She was becoming more well-known for her work helping abused women and children, but she was still pretty obscure. It was a fortunate opportunity she had been invited to speak about her programs on a national radio show. It just so happened Tina heard the broadcast and it sparked her interest. She contacted Rachel and invited her and her daughters to visit the Metcafe ranch in Tennessee.

Tina—better known as Katrina Metcafe—was Rachel's favorite female country singer. Rachel listened to her music on the radio almost every day. She was literally world-famous. Rachel had never dreamed of meeting—much less becoming friends with—the country artists she so admired. Rachel liked Katrina because of the poignant nature of her songs. Through her music, Tina addressed issues such as abuse and brought healing to hurting people.

Little did Rachel guess when Tina flew her to Tennessee that she would meet another of her country music favorites, Troy Keyton, or that her life would become inexplicably and permanently intertwined with his.

Tina, searching for a way to combine her interest in helping abused women with Rachel's efforts, invited their good friend and fellow musician Troy Keyton (whom Mike had years before nicknamed TJ) to join Rachel's family for dinner. Later, Rachel often teased Tina that she had been playing matchmaker all along. Tina always sheepishly denied it.

Chapter 4: Small Town

As Mike and Tina, with their two daughters, embraced Rachel and her girls into their lives, Rachel and TJ felt an immediate attraction. It didn't take long for all of them to feel like family. Even before Rachel knew she and TJ would marry, she knew Tina would remain one of her best friends. It was the kind of friendship that was more like sisterhood. The kids referred to themselves as cousins and all the adults were called aunt or uncle. Being short on extended family, Rachel soaked it up.

Mike had been Tina's producer, business manager and side-kick as well as husband. They were now retired, but it was highly unlikely that any of them—TJ and Rachel included—would ever really stop working. Retirement from the music industry just meant more time to work on projects that served hurting people.

Rachel greeted Tina with a big hug. Any opportunity to be together she embraced wholeheartedly. Mike was solid and steady, balancing Tina's artistic, whimsical personality. Their oldest daughter, Laney, was Beth's best friend and they had attended Ole Miss together. Although Mike was not Laney's biological father, she was very much like him—steady, smart and goodhearted. Now Laney lived in South Carolina with her husband and two very busy little girls.

The Metcafe's younger daughter, Annie, the spitting image of her mother and with just as much spirit, was in her last year of university in Europe. Tina and Mike had just gotten back from visiting her.

While Mike teased Beth about her husband and kids being absent, Rachel and Tina lost no time catching up. The atmosphere among the friends was relaxed and jovial.

"Uncle Mike, you are so funny," Beth answered sarcastically. "I just don't know how you can live with him, Aunt Tina."

"Oh, he is pretty tough to take, but we manage." She rolled her eyes. "I thought about leaving him in Europe, but he begged me to keep him."

"I see how it is," Mike said. Before he got seated he pointed to Steve. "Too many girls here, Steve. Maybe you and I should head down to the field. I think TJ's got the right idea." Steve grinned and nodded in agreement. Rachel chided Mike about needing to catch his breath from the long hike up the stairs.

"Aren't you a bit old to be going up and down or pacing the sidelines?" she joked.

"You'd better learn to respect your elders, young lady." He shook his finger at her, pretending to pout. "I'm here to watch my fake nephew play football." He motioned to Steve to join him. "There is entirely too much estrogen up here. I

Chapter 4: Small Town

don't think I could concentrate."

Rachel knew his protests were bogus. He wanted to stand along the fence to feel part of the game with TJ and the other fathers.

As he started down the bleachers, Tina grabbed his hand. "Hey! If you all are going down there would you mind getting me a sweet tea?"

Mike rolled his eyes again and looked at Rachel. "What about you Cowgirl?" That was the nickname he had given Rachel before she had married TJ. "Soda or sweet tea?"

Rachel returned his warm smile and shook her head. Her hands were full with the little ones and the closer to game time the more nervous she felt. She sure didn't need a caffeine rush to kick in with her adrenaline.

Mike kissed his wife and he and Steve headed down to get drinks and goodies for the kids before hanging out with the guys along the sidelines.

Rachel nudged her friend. She had noticed Tina watching Mike with intensity. "Still turn you head?" she asked.

"You know, Rache, when your kids are gone you kind of connect in a new way. At least we have." Tina smiled and blushed a little. "Maybe it's 'cause we finally have time to really enjoy just the two of us. I already had Laney when we started dating, then we had Annie right away. After that, of course, we had all those years on the road. I think this is the first time we've had a moment to ourselves. And let me tell you—" She leaned close to Rachel's ear and whispered. "—that man has not lost his sex appeal."

"TMI!" Rachel shook her arms with mock embarrassment. "No, seriously, Tina, this is why you two are our role models. We hope to love each other the way you and Mike do when we have been married over twenty years." Rachel pointed to her kids and whispered loudly, "But we have heard it from our kids—affection shown by your parents, especially after the age of fifty, is 'gross' and I think they even used the word 'annoying.'" They both giggled. Beth and Hope were the ones to roll their eyes this time.

As Mike and Steve came back with drinks, popcorn and a ton of candy, the game was starting. Steve apologized to Hope for the candy, telling her he couldn't control Mike. "He's a grandpa gone bad!" he chuckled. Hope shook her head. "Honest Hope, I tried to tell him he was getting me in trouble."

"Oh, that's fine." She turned to Tina. "We are sending the kids home with you and Uncle Mike tonight."

Tina laughingly gestured for Steve to hide the candy, but Mike didn't notice. He was watching the kick off and would never know. Tina snatched a few goodies and stuffed them

Chapter 4: Small Town

into her purse.

Rachel noticed Ben was not starting, but he had his helmet on and was standing near Coach Fischer, ready to be sent in. Kyle, not in uniform, stood next to TJ. Rachel figured TJ was keeping Kyle close and out of trouble. Having to miss the first game—a home game—would be tough for any kid. While Kyle's consequence was well-deserved, TJ must have sensed his hostility. He would keep Kyle engaged during the game by standing close and talking to him about the plays—anything to help him ride it out. Rachel said a quick prayer for Kyle.

Part way through the second quarter, Emily showed up with a couple of her guy friends. Heritage was playing well. They looked much stronger than the opposing team. Ben was still waiting for the opportunity to get in the game. Emily pointed out her dad and brother to her friends. As she passed, she called loudly to her brother and waved to TJ.

Rachel couldn't remember Emily's friends' names, but she remembered their behavior. She wasn't fond of most of Emily's new friends. They seemed loud and obnoxious, caring about little besides the next party. Or so it appeared to Rachel.

Emily and her small band of followers took seats nearby. She gave a quick hug and a cheerful hello to Hope and Beth before gathering her nieces into a big bear hug. The two little girls squealed with delight. Tina got a hug, too. Rachel smiled at the cheerful reunion. Emily saved her for last. Despite her reservations about the company Emily kept, Rachel was glad to see her. She always brought so much energy to any situation. Similar to Rachel, she exuded zeal and passion for whatever she believed in. Seeing her at this moment among family and friends, Rachel realized how much she missed having Emily home.

Emily introduced Jake and Bill. Rachel leaned forward to catch their names. She remembered Jake as the drummer in Emily's band, but she wasn't sure what Bill did. She hoped Emily wasn't dating him. Before going on the road, Emily had always been pretty level-headed about guys she chose to date. Again, Rachel felt uneasy about Emily's new lifestyle.

At half time, Heritage was up by two touchdowns, and Ben had still not played. The coach had moved other offensive players into Kyle and Ben's positions. He must have felt it was too big a risk to play an inexperienced freshman.

The cheerleaders and pep team took the field for their mid-game show. Rachel stood to stretch her legs. She saw the team heading to the locker room. TJ followed behind the group with a few of the boys, including Kyle. He looked up at the stands and waved to Rachel and the other family members.

Chapter 4: Small Town

Hope also stood, getting ready to leave. The little girls were worn out and getting fussy. Rachel helped her gather up toys and books. Steve came sprinting up the steps and took the diaper bag from Hope who looked as tired as the children. Rachel hugged her and the grandchildren and watched them make their way to ground level. They said good-bye to Mike while the girls bounced up and down, crying that they didn't get to say good-bye to "Papa." Hope reassured them they would see Papa on Sunday and get to play with him then.

Ricky had been sitting in the bleachers with friends from school, but he came by at half-time to ask for some money to buy food. He was surprised when he noticed Emily. Taking one of the spots Hope's family had vacated, Rick settled in next to Emily for the second half. Rachel overheard Rick giving his sister a hard time about not coming home often enough.

"What? Are you too famous for us now?" he chided.

"Oh, did you miss me, little brother?" she teased.

Rick just shrugged as though he could care less. But Rachel knew he did miss having his sisters around. Rick was a people person through and through. He loved being part of the family and didn't like it when they were apart. If Emily or one of the other girls failed to keep in touch through Facebook, texting, messages or calling, it was usually Rick who mentioned to Rachel that he hadn't heard from them in a while. Sometimes Rachel wondered if his diligence in keeping tabs on everyone was because he had lost so many people as a young child. Maybe he felt responsible to make sure it didn't happen again.

The last couple years it had become nearly impossible for the entire family to come together for holidays or other special events. This bothered Rick more than anyone else. He also was most affected when it came time to his sisters and their families to go home after a visit. When he was younger he would melt into tears and be unsettled for days. As he got older and realized they would come back it was a little easier, but still he struggled with it. He would mope and be irritable afterward.

As Emily and Rick jibed each other, a long-time friend, Tucker, stopped by. In high school, Tucker had been close buddies with Gracie's husband, Danny. Though only twenty-five, Tucker had recently been named director of Hope Enterprises, the umbrella organization that ran the various ministries Rachel had started in Colorado and Tennessee. TJ had put together the organization and expanded it to a national level. Tucker was like a son to TJ after years of participation in their outreaches and camps. Tucker and Danny had been the first teens TJ had mentored. Tucker had a good head and big heart. As Rachel watched him greeting everyone, she saw how comfortable he was with the family.

"Hey, Tucker. How's it going?" Rachel said as he took a seat beside her.

"Hi, Mrs. Keyton, Mrs. Metcafe." He stretched his arm across Rachel to shake Tina's hand. "It's been a busy week." He inquired about the game and whether Ben had gotten to play. They chatted a few minutes about a group of boys from the mentoring project coming to the farm to work with the horses. Tucker had an ease about him. Rachel noted that he was also a nice-looking kid. Finally, he excused himself to visit with Emily.

Rachel and Tina listened as Emily and her friends talked with him about music and their tour schedule. Eventually, the conversation turned to Tucker's work. The group became suddenly serious. Tucker had recently set up a program for kids in juvenile corrections to get mentoring services and therapy. Stories of what the kids had done and what had been done to them seemed to startle Tucker's captive audience until the football team came rushing back onto the field.

The crowd cheered and clapped. Rachel stood and waved. Ben looked toward the stands and waved back. It was a quick one, but at least he acknowledged his family. As was customary for him, he acted like he didn't care if anyone was there to watch him. It was part of being a teenager—

and part of being Ben—to maintain a hard exterior, giving little indication of the value to him of how much others cared about him. Rachel knew better though. He didn't hide it as well as the thought. Rachel could see that he cared deeply that his entire family did everything they could to make it to his games. It didn't matter if he played or not; they could not reassure him too much about their commitment to him.

The game was uneventful. Heritage held their lead for their expected win. Ben went into the game for the final five minutes. He made no great plays, scored no points, but he got playing time, earning him a varsity letter as a freshman. Rachel and the entire family were on their feet, cheering wildly.

When Ben came off the field the Keyton family along with the Metcafes were there to congratulate him. As everyone told him how proud they were, Ben was trying hard to remain aloof, but his smile kept taking over. Rachel didn't embarrass him with big hugs. She held back a bit, watching her family surrounding him. Finally, he broke free to go to the locker room. He glanced at Rachel and she gave him a huge smile and two thumbs up. He flashed a quick grin and walked away with what could only be described as a swagger.

CHAPTER 5
I Didn't Know It at the Time

It was late, yet no one wanted to call it a night. Rachel invited everyone to come over to the farm for ice cream. Mike and Tina, Emily and her friends, Beth and Laney eagerly agreed. It wasn't unusual after a game for everyone to head over to the Keytons or the Metcafes. Rachel knew TJ and Mike would spend at least an hour going over each and every play. The plans were made as they waited for Ben to finish up in the locker room.

When Ben and TJ came out the family was hanging around the parking lot. Ben was again engulfed. Rachel and TJ stood back and watched. Rachel reached for TJ"s hand, but instead, he put his arm around her and pulled her close. He kissed the top of her head. She smiled up at him and leaned in to his embrace.

"Good game, huh?" he beamed.

"Yep," she agreed. "Not sure what is more fun—the game or seeing everyone support Ben like this."

"I know. Rache, I am so proud of our family." Arm in arm, they started toward their vehicles. "Seems like the boys are in a good place, doesn't it?" Before Rachel could reply, Ben and Rick sought them out.

"Hey, Dad?"

Rachel and TJ stopped so Ben could talk to them. "Some kids from the team asked me to go with them to celebrate our first home game. They even said Rick could come. Can we go?"

He'd asked TJ, but he gave Rachel a pleading look. Rick had the same eager expression, his eyes begging for a yes.

Instantly, Rachel felt ill at ease. Allowances were often made, but in general, they had family rules about planning things in advance. The football team was a pretty good group of kids, but Ben and Rick were the youngest of the group. Of all the kids, the boys needed structure and guidelines the most. Transitions, changes in plans and new situations were still areas they struggled with. Rachel could feel TJ tense. He looked at her to get her read on the situation.

Rachel shrugged her shoulders. TJ bit his lower lip on one side. He was thinking out his questions carefully. He asked which kids were going and what they were going to do. Ben was able to name a few of the boys, but he didn't have any information about where they were going. The girls had learned in similar situations to give as many details as possible, but the boys hadn't yet learned what their parents

Chapter 5: I Didn't Know It at the Time

needed to know. Rachel knew her sons had a much more difficult time communicating any plan. From homework projects to particulars about their day, Rachel found it like pulling teeth to get enough or even the correct information.

Watching TJ now, she could see him getting a little annoyed. It wasn't that he didn't want to give permission. They often told the boys, "Help me say yes. Give me information so I can agree with your plans." With the girls, it had always been about safety. With the boys, TJ and Rachel were still trying to find balanced ways to grant more and more freedom.

"How can we say yes if you don't even know anything about it?" TJ asked.

Rick jumped in. "I can find out. Some of the guys are right over there." He pointed eagerly.

"Alright, then. Let's go talk to them."

Rachel appreciated TJ's directness. He led her by the hand as they followed Rick to the group of kids. Ben looked embarrassed to have both his mother and father talking to his teammates. Nonetheless, he went along with it, a true testament to how badly he wanted to go.

After asking several questions, TJ found out the kids were going to a pizza restaurant near the school. Those were the only definite plans. The rest would be formulated as they went along. That wasn't going to work for Ben or Rick. Rachel could see TJ wasn't going along with it.

They pulled Rick and Ben aside so they could talk about it. Rachel expressed her concerns about who was driving and where they were going after pizza. Ben kept looking at the ground, refusing eye contact, already upset. He kicked at the dirt with the toe of one shoe. Rachel knew how much he hated asking for anything, especially permission to do something. In general, he tended to have a pessimistic attitude about any decision to be made. So he was gearing himself up for whatever he thought the worse outcome would be.

Rachel asked him to look at her. He reluctantly raised his head. "Ben, we aren't saying no," she affirmed. "We just need more of a game plan here."

He mumbled something that sounded like he knew that. But he had already dropped his head again.

"Yeah, whatever," he muttered. He continued to kick at the dirt.

Rachel silently implored TJ as if willing him to intervene. It wasn't lost on TJ. They had gotten pretty good at tag-teaming their united front with the boys. TJ stepped in right on cue.

"Hey, Son, how about I take you guys over to the pizza

Chapter 5: I Didn't Know It at the Time

place and you all can hang out there and eat and whatnot? I won't come in. I can give you an hour, then we can go on home. I am totally fine with the pizza plan. I just am not crazy about the rest of it."

Rick was enthusiastic about TJ's suggestion and eagerly agreed. Ben looked at his dad with a defiant, hard glint in his eyes. Compromise was not his strong suit. Rachel braced herself for the storm she saw brewing.

"So, we can go get pizza, but that's it?" he asked curtly.

"Yep. That is my offer. You can go out with the guys and eat, but when they are done, you come home."

Ben shook his head and kicked at the dirt more roughly.

"What, Ben?" TJ asked. "What is it you want?"

"I don't know. It's just, I don't know how long they are going to be there. And I don't like it that I have to be picked up by my parents like a little kid." He threw his hands up, exasperated. "Why can't we just go with everyone else and then get a ride home?"

"Because," TJ explained again patiently, "we don't have any of the information we need to make any other decision." TJ looked at Ben's disgruntled posture and he stepped a little closer to the boy. "Ben, your choices are to go with your friends to pizza and then come home or to come home now."

Rick also stepped in close to his brother. "Come on, Ben. It will be fun. Next game we can figure out stuff ahead of time." Rick was practically pleading. Rachel could see Ben was getting more agitated. She knew Rick saw it, too. Ben didn't look willing to back down without a fight. His fists were clenched and his body tense. She had seen this look a million times. He would rather go without anything than give in.

Ben pushed Rick slightly, gaining some space. His eyes darted to Rachel and then to the family group nearby. Waiting for Ben to work through a transition was a familiar phenomenon their family had been through many times.

Finally, Ben locked scowling eyes with TJ. Both of them looked determined, eyes hard and dark. Rick took a step back toward Rachel. She hoped her face was calm and neutral. They had come a long way since the early days when a moment like this was an hour-long tantrum. While Ben might not fling himself on the floor as did when he was six, Rachel knew he was every bit as capable of disrupting any possibility of a plan he found unfair. His rage tended to be more verbal as he got older, although he had lost the door to his room numerous times for slamming it. His teenage-sized tantrums usually ended when he became sullen or refused to interact.

Rachel also knew TJ was going to hold steady and there

Chapter 5: I Didn't Know It at the Time

was no way he would back down. She held her breath and prayed silently for both TJ and Ben. Having been an angry young man himself, TJ battled his own emotions when his son fought for control and power. He rubbed his hand on his chin and took a half step back, softening his stance, and exhaled slowly. "Son? Up to you. What'll it be?"

Ben glanced away and then back at TJ. TJ shrugged his shoulders and stepped back a little more.

"Oh, my God!" Ben was disgusted and angry. "What do you think is going to happen?"

TJ stood his ground, doing his best to remain docile as he waited for Ben to give him an answer. Ben, unwilling to yield, glared at him defiantly.

Finally, in a last ditch effort to avoid compromise, he shouted, "Fine. If I can't go do what I want I am going home." Ben turned to Rick. "You can go if you want Rick—be a baby and have your daddy pick you up." He stomped away, past the family waiting by the cars, and haughtily threw his stuff into the back of TJ's Jeep.

Rick was crushed. Rachel didn't know whether to go after Ben or talk with Rick. TJ gave her an exasperated look. She mouthed back, "I know."

"Look, Rache, I'll take Ben home. If you want to take

Rick with the group going for pizza, maybe Tina will go with you."

Rick interrupted the plan. "Nah, I don't want to go anymore."

"Are you sure, Honey?" Rachel felt bad for him. She motioned for TJ to go on ahead and see to Ben so she could talk with Rick. She asked him to send everyone on their way.

"Hey, Son, want to take a walk?"

He shook his head. "I just want to go home."

Rachel wasn't sure what was going through his mind. "Are you sure?"

He nodded. She and Rick walked quietly to the SUV. "Rick, you can still go if you want. I can take you."

"It's okay, Mom. I don't mind going home and being with everyone there." He opened his door and started to get into the passenger seat. "I really don't want to go if Ben isn't going."

Rachel tried to read his expression. She couldn't tell what he was feeling. "You don't always have to go along with Ben. He made his choice, but it doesn't have to be yours."

Rick shrugged, but didn't say anything.

Chapter 5: I Didn't Know It at the Time

Rachel paused. She didn't start the car. She thought about how excited Rick had been to be invited to go with the guys. Rick was bright, friendly and sensitive. Being Ben's younger brother wasn't the easiest thing. There were many times Rick naturally allowed Ben to lead, even if it meant he had to step aside. She had often witnessed him before deliberately let Ben be better at a video game or win an argument. Both she and TJ encouraged Rick to say what he wanted and to find himself. Rick was a peacekeeper.

"Mom?" Rick pulled her back into the present.

She turned to face him. "Yeah, Honey?"

"I'm really okay with not going out with everyone. I'm not lying about wanting to go home. It's okay."

"Rick, you are super sweet, but it seemed like earlier you really wanted to go."

"I did want to go, but just to be with Ben and his friends. It isn't really my thing."

"You looked so upset when Ben chose not to go."

"I was bummed. I hate it when he does that. He is the one that really wanted to go. But then it's like it is his will against Dad's and it never ends good. They just end up both pissed off. Why does he do that?"

"Who? Ben or Dad?"

Rick gave a short laugh. "Both of them. Can't you see how stubborn they both are?" Rick looked at her. Thinking about TJ and Ben facing off, posturing like two dominate males, Rachel gave a little chuckle, too. It was true. Ben was always about gaining power and control. When he was younger, it had been more directed at Rachel. Back in the day TJ had been his hero and could do no wrong. But lately, the taller Ben got, the more he seemed to butt heads with TJ. Rachel could see it took TJ off guard at times. Ben was his first son. He had troubles with his daughters, but Rachel knew there was nothing like the power struggles between a parent and child of the same sex, especially when the child was very much like you.

"You're right, Rick. They both are stubborn. Not a bad trait for them to share. It must be hard for you though to watch them butt heads like that." Rick nodded. Rachel was reminded how much Rick hated conflict. She was fully aware of his deep fear of people getting upset or angry. There was no way she could protect him from conflicts, nor would she if she could. Living in a big household with lots of emotions and real-life relationships playing out daily had helped him learn to trust his family to handle frustration, anger and conflict appropriately. But still, having been unsettled easily by others' battles as a child, Rachel had a lot of empathy for her younger son.

Chapter 5: I Didn't Know It at the Time

Rachel quietly reminded Ricky that his dad understood Ben's anger and he would do the right thing. Rick agreed with her but then he reminded her that Ben wasn't so good at backing off.

"Yes," she said. "I can see that your daddy and your brother have a lot in common. But really, Ricky, I don't think it can always be your job to give up what you want to keep the peace. That worries me, too." They had had this conversation before.

"I know, Mama, but really, this time I was just going to hang with Ben and his friends. Can we please go home? Besides, Emily is at home, and Tucker too."

There were so many more things Rachel wanted to say. She loved it when they had time like this to just talk, but she had the good sense to understand that kids were usually done with the conversation before adults. "You bet," she said and smiled.

"Do you think Emily will still be there when we get back?"

"Hmmm. I hope so."

CHAPTER 6
From Ricky's Journal

When people ask me about being adopted they usually ask if Ben is my real brother or if my sister is my real sister. They ask, "What about your mother, is she your real mother?" I guess they mean my birth mother. I don't think of my birthmother as my real mama. And just so you know, that sort of questions are really annoying. This family—my family—is the most real thing I have.

Yes, Ben is my real blood brother and I don't remember ever being without him as a central part of my life, but the love I have for my sisters is just as real. When Mary teases me or Emily is having a hard time, it is my real family. I might have the same blood as Ben, but that doesn't make him more real.

The truth is, I don't remember too much about my birth family, just some vague empty feelings mixed with a deep down fear when I try to picture our other mother. Ben, he remembers a lot more than I do. For a long time, he was pretty mad about everything, even being adopted. He is still plenty mad about the things that happened to us. Once he told me about how he had to protect me from getting hit by her and how he used to try to stop her from drinking. He has actual scars from times she hurt him. I'm glad I don't remember.

What I do remember is that from the time I came to this house I felt like people cared about me. You might think a 4 or 5 year-old boy wouldn't really get that. But I think little kids can know when they are safe. At first, maybe it was the stark difference between the absence of love or belonging and the acceptance and care of coming here. When I got here I was young, but I remember feeling understood and wanted. That is how it was for me.

Don't get me wrong. There were times I had my fears and doubts, times I thought they might get tired of us and send me and Ben back (back where, I'm not sure). I remember when I used to get really scared that Ben would get us both in trouble. He seems to like keep things stirred up when I am all about keeping everything calm. I still feel scared when he gets into fights at school or at football. I still have a tough time when people get really upset, or if there is a lot of yelling.

I hate it when my sisters fight or when Ben and Dad are angry. I feel all tense when my parents get into "discussions" and sound like they are arguing. Mama is good about reassuring me and I am learning that this is family, too—to

Chapter 6: From Rickey's Journal

have a safe place to even be mad or upset. But I still don't like it. Even on TV it bothers me if there is too much tension between the characters. Weird, I know.

My mama, she is good at understanding this stuff. I still worry about Ben, but I know my parents can handle him. Just like how she could tell I was really scared and she helped me to feel safe, she is also really good with Ben. I watch Mama with Ben. He used to kick and scream and stomp around his room, and she'd just sit near him. She wouldn't ask him questions like a lot of adults, she would just talk quietly to him until he would finally calm down enough to sit in her lap or cry. I knew that if Ben was safe with her, then I was, too.

My dad, he is great. He is more forceful than Mama and it took me a while to trust him. He didn't sit with us when we were upset and he isn't the same kind of calm, but he is safe. There were lots of times he would just hold onto Ben to keep him from hurting anyone or himself. When we were little he would take us out to the lake on the back of the property and we could throw rocks in the water and he would just be there with us. Other times he would take us out to the ball field and let Ben and me hit baseballs until we were worn out.

I remember one time Ben was super mad about something—I don't even remember what—and Dad took him for a ride to the lake. It was when we first started living here and I guess I was worried about what he was going to do to Ben, so I begged to go. Maybe he knew I needed to be there. I usually stay pretty close to Ben when he gets upset. Anyway, we went to the lake. We got out and Dad told Ben to go ahead and yell, scream and holler. Ben refused at first, I remember that. But then Dad just kept encouraging him to tell the trees and the whole woods what it was he was so mad about.

"I got plenty I am mad about for you, Son," he said. And then he hollered really loud, "I hate it that other people hurt Ben!" I think that scared Ben a little and maybe he didn't want Dad to yell anymore. It scared me when he yelled. But Ben finally said something and Daddy kept telling him to go ahead and say it louder. Pretty soon they were both screaming at the top of their lungs about the awful stuff that had happened to us. I just watched for a long time. I think I was scared to hear it. Then Ben started to cry. Back then, my brother never cried.

He sobbed, "I hate it that I can't forget what she did to me!" And that was when Daddy just knelt down with him and held onto him. I think he was crying, too. I know I was. I came over and Daddy pulled me in and we stayed there for a while and cried. Maybe that is when things started getting better for Ben.

Chapter 6: *From Rickey's Journal*

When we used to go to this counselor guy, he told us sometimes sad stuff would turn to mad. I think mine stays hurt and sad, but I am okay talking about it. I guess with Ben, his sad really turns to mad. He thinks about things a lot, and maybe it just bounces around in him, but me, I actually don't think too much about it.

He plays sports hard and I think it helps him, but I tend to like being with friends and laughing. Mostly I think we are feeling better because of this family. And so what I am supposed to say when someone asks if this is my real family? Seems pretty real to me.

CHAPTER 7
Get Off My Back

By the time Rachel got back to the house with Rick everyone else had already arrived at the farm. The big yellow house was lit up with activity. Rachel loved the warmth of coming home to their immense colonial home. When Rick saw all the cars in the driveway he declared with child-like glee, "Looks like a party!"

Rachel recognized the Metcafe's car and of course, there was Beth's Prius and Tucker's Ford truck. Parked haphazardly and blocking her access to the garage was an old beat-up truck she didn't recognize. She parked off to the side. Rick eagerly jumped out. He couldn't wait to see everyone.

As soon as Rachel got out of the car Emily came running, headed straight toward her. "Mom! You have to stop him!" She was shouting dramatically, waving her arms. "He is ruining everything!" She stomped her foot. Emily was nothing if not theatrical.

Rick tried to say hello to her, even asked her what was going on, but she blew right past him. He watched her a moment, a brief look of hurt when she didn't acknowledge him, then headed into the house. Rachel heard a muttered, "Whatever."

Rachel felt irritated and exhausted. She never liked it when the kids met her by the car in this manner. She had a rule about at least getting into the house before they started unloading on her. She sighed. It was already late and any hope of a quiet visit with friends was fading. She had presumed TJ and Mike would have Ben calmed down by now. She wasn't sure she had the patience to deal with whatever was sending Emily into the latest uproar.

Rachel glanced at her watch. She took a deep breath and willed herself to respond with all the composure she could. She reminded herself how Emily, like her, met life with unbounded enthusiasm. She and Emily were the ones that would come up with plans and were the most likely to carry them out. But unlike Rachel, Emily was also very vocal about her thoughts and feelings and she tended to be quite opinionated about the way she thought things should be.

This scene with Emily meeting her on her way into the house had been played out many times in the past. Typically, it was to tell Rachel every detail of what she had missed while she'd been away from the house. Unfortunately, it was also to tell Rachel what the other kids had done before anyone else could have the chance. There were times, especially when the kids were all younger, it felt as though they were

Chapter 7: Get Off My Back

dancing circles around her like a May Pole. She remembered how frustrating it was when they argued about who got to tell which part of the story. It had been a while since those days. The boys rarely fought over who got to talk first.

When the girls were all home Rachel had established a ten-minute rule. No one could ask her anything the first ten minutes in the house. She had to get in, put things away, and sometimes use the toilet first. Emily's behavior tonight brought a rush of memories Rachel had no desire to revisit. Emily was no less dramatic than she'd been in junior high. Here she was rushing out to meet Mom with the latest crisis. By the sounds of it, it was to tattle on her dad. Rachel was surprised how the irritation this kind of behavior used to cause was immediately present.

Rachel paused to gain composure then quietly asked her daughter what was going on. Emily was oblivious to Rachel's efforts to calm her. She continued to rant about TJ and the unfairness of it all.

Well, Rachel thought, at least whatever was going on it had nothing to do with Ben. Apparently a lot had transpired during her few moments with Rick. Rachel tried to move past Emily toward the house without further annoying her daughter.

"Mom!" Emily had a sharp edge to her voice, bringing

Rachel back to attention. "Are you seriously going to just let Dad tell my friends everything he thinks they are doing wrong with their lives?" Emily threw up her arms, aggravated and frustrated. Tears threatened to take over as they often did with Emily in moments of passion.

"Honey, I have no idea what is going on. I haven't even gotten into the house yet. Maybe you should let me go in and see for myself?" Rachel suggested. But Emily was beyond that kind of reasoning.

"No, Mom. Really, you have to help me here! I get home and Dad just starts right in with Jake and Bill. He doesn't like them. It isn't fair." She was literally shaking. If she hadn't looked so miserable Rachel would have laughed. Emily continued her tirade about TJ's unreasonable behavior and something about Uncle Mike being just as bad. Rachel had her doubts about who was unreasonable, but she was finally able to move around Emily and reach the house.

"Fine, go in!" Emily yelled. "I know you are going to side with Daddy. You always do." Rachel shook her head. It wasn't the first time Rachel had heard those words from one of their six girls.

"Honestly, Emily, it's like you are thirteen again." Rachel surprised herself with how provoked she was. "For goodness sake, would you please calm down?" She opened the door

Chapter 7: Get Off My Back

then turned back to face Emily. "Maybe you should stay out here for a while. Take a walk down to the barn and get hold of yourself. Come in after you have your emotions under control."

There was no way Emily was going to leave the action; it just wasn't in her. She shook her head, protesting violently against the idea. She stomped past Rachel into the house. As she did, Rachel smelled alcohol. No wonder Emily was being so irrational. Rachel took a deep breath, trailing Emily through the kitchen and onto the back patio, knowing she was heading straight into the heat of battle.

Tina and Mike were seated off to the left and waved timidly to Rachel. The two band members, Jake and Bill, were perched uncomfortably near the door. They looked ready to escape at any moment. TJ stood directly in front of them, leaning slightly against the patio table, his arms crossed and his face stern. This was his heavy-duty disapproving parental expression.

Rachel hesitated in the doorway for a second, not sure she wanted to join the fray. TJ glanced at her and she caught the weariness in his eyes. He refocused his attention on the two young men.

She considered retreating to check on Rick and Ben. The energy on the deck was charged with tension. On the other side of Mike and Tina, Beth waved her over. Rachel stepped into the cool night air. She didn't see Tucker or Mary and figured they were playing pool downstairs or upstairs on the X-Box with Ben and Rick.

Rachel acknowledged Beth, but chose, rather, to stand close to TJ. As nonchalantly as she could, she asked loud enough for everyone to hear what was going on. No one said anything for a moment. Rachel looked from face to face. Finally, TJ gave her some details. Emily and her friends had been drinking. They had arrived shortly before Rachel and Rick, apparently after stopping along the way for more beer or to get high.

"Beer bottles in hand, already high on something before they even got here, they were weaving just walking up." He pointed to the young men. "I told them we don't drink out here on the farm and reminded Emily how unacceptable that was. Then this one—" He pointed to the dark-haired kid named Bill. "—he forcefully disagreed with our no-alcohol policy. Tried pushing Mike around when we took their bottles." Rachel looked at Mike who nodded. TJ continued, "Oh, and did you know, he is also dating our daughter?" TJ shook his head, giving Emily a look of disappointment as if he still could not believe it. "I never figured you to go for the pot-head, loser type, Em."

"You don't even know him, Dad!" Emily protested, incensed and tearful.

Chapter 7: Get Off My Back

"Yeah, you know, you're right. I don't. But Emily, I know this stuff." He pointed at the bottles of beer on the table behind him. "I've been there before. I know all about the music business and climbing your way to the top; how a little bit of fame can destroy you. And I know you. Come on, Em. You are better than this. At least, you used to be."

Emily didn't say anything. Rachel watched her face as she took in her father's words. Rachel could see that despite Emily's anger, she was embarrassed at this conflict. Emily respected TJ, and Tina too. Both of them were once highly-sought-after artists. Their music had not died out even though they were retired. Their reputations in the business were esteemed. Troy Keyton's high standards were legendary.

Emily knew all about TJ's past. Rachel had been part of numerous talks TJ had had with Emily over the years about values and ethics, self-respect, and what it meant in terms of this particular business. Outwardly, Emily was holding onto her pride, but Rachel knew deep down she cared what TJ and her Aunt Tina thought about her—she cared a lot.

The guys, Jake and Bill, weren't sober, but they were coherent enough to hang their heads and back down. Rachel could see they realized too late they had perhaps made a mistake in coming out to the farm tonight. It had to be embarrassing to face two of the most famous, well-known and well-traveled country music artists in recent history. In different circumstances they might even have been a little star-struck.

Rachel took it all in, and silently prayed. Judging by how tired and worn down they all looked, she hoped things were going to be wrapped up soon. Emily, however, embarrassed and hurt at TJ's disappointment in her, was still fuming. She used her anger to mask her own shame. Emily lacked the maturity to admit her error in judgment. She wasn't going to humble herself enough to back down. She stood in front of TJ, her hands clenched as she bitterly looked at the faces of her family. TJ kept his gaze steady. He didn't challenge her, but he wasn't going to back down either.

Rachel could see the concern, the love, and the compassion of their close friends and family. She knew with Emily's impaired judgment she might not realize all the most important adults in her life were sitting in front of her, seeing her in a less-than-shining moment. Rachel couldn't rescue her, but she wondered if there was a way to allow Emily off the hook for now. It wasn't going to do much good to continue to confront her in this particular moment.

Rachel moved to her daughter's side and pulled her as close as Emily would allow. There wasn't much give on Emily's part, but she didn't pull away. She stood stiffly while Rachel put her arm around her shoulder. TJ looked at the two of them, rubbed his chin and bit one side of his bottom lip. The tension was waning a little.

Chapter 7: Get Off My Back

"So," Rachel began slowly and then said lightly, "sounds like I didn't miss too much."

Tina chuckled softly. Rachel chose her words carefully. "I am sure you guys can understand that we have our house rules here for our own reasons." She waited, trying to catch either Bill's or Jake's eye, but they didn't look up. "I know you all are adults and can do what you want and I am sure you will. But you know, here at our house, we keep it pretty clear and simple. No alcohol, no drugs. Basically, we are G-rated. I am certain Emily told you."

Rachel paused again. She knew full well Emily had fallen short on telling anyone about her upbringing or household rules. She raised her eyebrow at Emily. "So while we respect your choices for your lives, we draw the line at what you choose to bring here. This is our safe place, our home."

Rachel stopped, giving time for her words to sink in. She could feel Emily next to her start to protest. But Rachel had more to say. Not giving Emily a chance to respond, she continued. "I am sure you guys can respect our position." She smiled as warmly as she could when the two young men looked up at her. "We figured most of our friends and family know how we do things around here. Our 'no alcohol' policy isn't going to change. We like our rules and our values. I am sure you heard this already from the others here, but I wanted to say it, too."

Rachel pulled Emily closer. "This is our home and our family. And like it or not, Emily is part of that." Emily struggled to pull away and Rachel let her go.

It was quiet on the deck. Rachel prayed silently for the impact of this encounter on these young lives. Finally, Mike and Tina stood together as if on cue.

"Well, we need to get home and hit the hay," Mike said. "But by the looks of it, you two—" He pointed to Bill and Jake. "—need a place to go tonight, so you can come with us. Same rules apply for our house, but right now you boys need a place to sleep it off. We don't want you driving, so go grab your stuff and come with us."

Jake looked at Bill who was looking at Emily. "Alright, I guess." Bill said. "Are you coming, Em?"

Before she could say anything both TJ and Mike stepped between them. TJ said it first: "No."

"Oh my God, Dad!" Emily said. "I can answer for myself. Maybe I want to stay with Bill."

"Like I am going to let that happen," Mike snickered. "Sorry, Sis. Tonight the open house is for these boys only. You all can see each other tomorrow. Let's go, men."

Rachel gave Tina a silent thank you as she passed. The guys sluggishly followed Mike and Tina to get their things out of their truck.

Chapter 7: Get Off My Back

Beth also stood to leave. "I'm going back to Nashville, Emily. You want to hang out at my apartment tonight?" Rachel knew Beth was giving Emily a way out, too.

"Anything is better than staying here." Emily stomped past TJ, Beth and Rachel as she, too, went to gather her necessities.

Beth gave TJ and Rachel a hug and said she would call or come by with Emily in the morning. Rachel thanked her for coming to the game. "Sorry it didn't go so well tonight."

Suddenly Rachel and TJ were alone on the patio. TJ heaved a sigh and turned to Rachel. He looked exhausted. She felt it, too.

"Well," he chuckled, "that went good."

Rachel didn't say anything for a second. Then the absurdity of the whole scene and how differently things had gone since the game ended hit her and she chortled. "You sure know how to throw an after-party, Mr. Keyton."

"Yeah, well, you are the one that cleared the room."

Then Rachel remembered the truck parked haphazardly in the driveway. "Oh dang, I couldn't get my car in the garage. I should have had them move their clunker."

"No worries, Babe." He dangled a set of keys. "I took

their keys right at the beginning. And that is what started the whole thing."

Rachel gave him a half smile and shrugged. He grinned at her. It was crazy what she felt for him. Touching his arm, she reached up and kissed him. He kissed her back and for a minute Rachel forgot her weariness. Finally, she pulled back slightly and TJ shook his head as if to clear it.

"Dang, woman! You are a major distraction."

"Just doing my part to keep the peace," she teased. Then she raised an eyebrow and jingled the keys he held.

"Okay, I'll go move cars around. I'm sure our boys, as well as Tucker and Mary, would appreciate knowing the conflict is over. I think they went into hiding as soon I started hollering."

"I'll go check on them and see if Tucker is even still here." Rachel's hand lingered on his arm. TJ patted her hand before they both moved apart, heading in different directions.

Rachel found Mary, Tucker and Ricky in the media room just off the kitchen on the main floor. The three of them were talking while a movie played quietly in the background. Rachel poked her head in. They stopped talking and looked up expectantly.

"Is Emily still here?" Rick asked hopefully.

Chapter 7: Get Off My Back

"She went with Beth back to her house," Rachel answered.

"Oh." Rick looked downcast. "I didn't even get to talk to her. Will she be back this weekend?"

Rachel told him she wasn't sure. She glanced over at Tucker and Mary. She supposed they were waiting to hear what finally happened. She gave them a little shrug. There wasn't much to tell. They probably knew more about the situation than she did.

"The guys went home with Uncle Mike and Aunt Tina. Like I said, Emily went home with Beth. She was still pretty upset with your daddy when she left. But I'm sure Beth will bring her by tomorrow." Rachel looked at the clock above the entertainment center. "It's really late, you guys. Probably better get to bed, right?"

Tucker jumped up. "Sorry Mrs. Keyton. I should be going." He looked down at Mary still seated on the couch. "Nice talking to you, Mary." He gave Rick a fist bump. "See ya, Ricky."

Rachel patted his back as he passed her. Mary got up to see him out. Rick stood and stretched.

"Did Ben already go to bed?" Rachel asked. She wondered how his mood was once he had gotten home.

"Yeah. He and Tucker were playing pool when I got here.

When the game was over, Mary and Tucker started talking about stuff, then he said he was tired and went to his room. He seemed pretty chill."

Rick stifled a yawn as he found the remote and turned off the TV. "I wasn't tired yet, so we decided to watch a movie. But instead, we ended up talking about Emily and Dad and stuff like that."

"Stuff like that, huh?" She put her hand on his arm and smiled at him. "You doing alright?" She knew how much he hated conflict and there had been plenty of that tonight.

"Yep. I'm good." He hugged her again, said good night and headed up the stairs. She debated following him to check on Ben, but decided against it. Ben was much more independent than Rick. Both of them were getting old enough that they didn't want her upstairs, let alone in their rooms tucking them in at night. Sometimes getting Ben to talk at all took all her therapy skills, and it wasn't going to happen in a late-night talk.

Yawning, Rachel started down the hall to turn off lights left on by the kids. Talking to Ben about the game would have to wait until tomorrow. She was too tired now anyway.

As she headed back to her room, Mary and TJ were coming in through the garage. Mary gave her dad a hug, and seeing Rachel, gave her one as well then said good night and went through the kitchen toward her little cottage. TJ grabbed a glass of water and turned off the kitchen lights. Rachel started getting ready for bed.

"I know you probably want to know what happened tonight," TJ said when he came into the bathroom where Rachel was brushing her teeth. She nodded, her mouth full of toothpaste. TJ exhaled noisily. He ran his hand through his hair. Rachel looked sideways at him, concerned.

"Rache, I don't know if I did the right thing." He sighed again, leaning against the counter. "When Emily walked in with those boys, smelling of alcohol and pot, in her own self-centered haze, I kind of lost it."

Rachel waited.

"I yelled at her in front of Mike and everyone. I basically told the boys to get out. I wasn't kind or rational. I don't know, Babe." He looked tired and discouraged but stood watching her.

Rachel rinsed her mouth and then cleaned her face. She dried her hands and face before turning toward him.

"Hey, TJ," she spoke sympathetically and moved close to where he leaned against the counter. She brushed his cheek with her fingertips. "It's going to be okay."

"Ya think?" He asked with a feeble grin, not masking his

discouragement. It was late and he looked just as tired as she felt. She nodded. He probably had been way over the top. When he could see it for himself, it was usually pretty bad. TJ was the first to admit he let his mouth run before he thought a lot of times. He had mellowed as he matured, but Rachel knew he struggled with tact. He wasn't threatening or violent, but he tended to cut straight to the point and didn't always choose his words carefully.

"Well, you might have to put a few dollars in the swear jar and mop up your mess with those kids, but I still love you." She said hoping to lighten his mood a little. TJ gave her a thin smile. More encouragingly, she added, "Besides, even if you did botch things tonight you have those guys' keys, so they will be back for another round. Thankfully, parenting isn't about being perfect. Family is messy if you do it right."

"Yep, that is for sure—plenty messy."

"But honestly, TJ, I am not sure it was a mistake. We have to draw a line somewhere on what we allow in our house. Emily knows that."

TJ agreed. They walked toward the bed. He finally smiled at her as he said, "This is a change."

Rachel gave him a questioning look, not understanding what he meant.

Chapter 7: Get Off My Back

"Well, usually I am an ass about something and you are telling me I need to knock it off." He snickered, seeing her objection. "No, I mean you do it in a loving way and all, but still—don't think I have ever had you tell me I wasn't too hard on 'em. Maybe I am getting soft in my old age."

"Could be," Rachel teased. "Or I am."

"Yeah, there's that." He drew her close to him, reached behind him to turn off the lamp then pulled up the covers. "Babe," he breathed into her hair, "no matter what those kids tell you about me, just keep in mind how good you feel right now." He kissed her unhurriedly.

"Fine, Hon," she whispered. "I got it. I won't believe a word they say."

CHAPTER 8
Better Than a Hallelujah

On Saturday, Rachel woke early, as she often did. She liked the way the house felt in the morning. She was a sunrise person who did her best thinking and praying in the early morning hours. Time alone helped her feel ready for the day. She could sit by the bay windows in the front room and write in her journal, Bible on her lap, and sip her coffee, focusing on matters of the heart.

As busy as the house had been the night before, it was now quiet, serene and peaceful. Rachel hoped it wasn't the calm before another storm. She fiddled with her pen, her mind replaying the events following the game. She considered Ben's attitude, and wondered what mood he would wake up in. Then her mind turned to Emily and all the drama surrounding her. What would it take for Emily to come home to her roots?

Emily was the most distant of the children. She was constantly on the road promoting her music. Rachel knew it was what she had to do to make her career work. But Emily was distant in more than miles. It wasn't only her life on the road that was in direct contrast to their family life. Emily was making choices that conflicted with the values she had been raised with. Even when she was not traveling Emily often chose to stay in Nashville with friends.

TJ and Rachel did their best to keep track of where she was. As much as possible they attended her shows. It was important to Rachel that Emily know they supported her. At times Emily appreciated their support; other times she pushed them away.

TJ kept close tabs on how Emily was doing and what was happening in the music industry. Rachel knew he worried about Emily. She also knew TJ didn't tell her everything he heard. He often talked with Emily privately about the reputation she was making for herself. Her shenanigans would certainly come up today. TJ wasn't shy about calling her on what he heard, and what he saw. Emily was bold enough to handle his straight talk. And she usually respected their family enough to avoid bringing her vices home.

Rachel and TJ had talked and prayed many restless nights about how best to guide her. While they felt strongly that for all the children's sakes they had to hold steady in their boundaries, they never wanted the kids to feel unwanted or unwelcomed. It was difficult to create a home full of safety and love without comprising what it meant to be home. They hoped Emily and the others as well would always know they could come home and be safe and nurtured. Both TJ and

Chapter 8: Better Than a Hallelujah

Rachel fought hard for balance between respecting their adult children's lives and keeping their home free from the undesirable influences.

TJ understood where Emily was coming from. When he was young and starting out in the business he had run with a wild crowd. Rachel had heard the stories. They were practically legend in Nashville. Likely, they flourished all the more because he later became so well-known for his solid family-man image and the stability in his life and music. Thankfully, TJ had good people around him. His first wife, Kris, and Tina and Mike helped his faith to grow. The road had been rocky and he really did not want Emily to travel the same path. Truth be told, he didn't want any of the kids to follow him into the music business.

Tina's road to fame offered a different perspective about country music. Like Emily, Tina grew up singing in church and with family. She never did became engulfed in the wild side of being on the road. She kept her family involved in every aspect of the business and held true to the values she grew up with. For years, her brother Tony played in her band and her father helped manage her career. Mike was her producer from the start.

Tina believed Emily was more grounded than Rachel gave her credit for. She maintained that Emily would come back to her roots before long. Rachel sure hoped so. Tina assured Rachel over and over that Emily could run, but she wouldn't get too far from God or family. Nonetheless, worry kept Rachel praying for the girl.

When Emily started her career, it had been tough to watch her battle to push her way into the music scene. She was never going to starve or be homeless like so many young artists trying to catch a break, but still there were long weeks of discouragement along the way. For Rachel, even more difficult than seeing Emily—or any of the kids—struggle to succeed was watching them thrash about spiritually. Emily was fighting against God and she had made it clear she wanted nothing to do with Him.

TJ and Rachel had raised their children with Christian values. They had worked hard to keep them involved in positive activities and around good kids, adults and families. While each of their children had to find their own way to a real relationship with God and their own moral compass, none of the girls except Emily had completely rejected their faith. Some had admittedly not felt close to God at times, but none had changed in the ways Emily had.

Growing up, Emily had always had a heart for worship and music was her mode of expressing her faith. For several years, at the end of high school and the first years of college, she had been part of the church worship team. But once she started traveling, staying up late on Saturday nights,

Chapter 8: Better Than a Hallelujah

she stopped going to church altogether. A number of times Rachel had asked her about worship and her relationship with God, but Emily didn't want to talk about it. She said she was fine and didn't want to be judged. So Rachel just prayed.

Ben was another one in a fight against faith. When he first came he had been willing to learn about Jesus. There were times he prayed the most heartfelt, tender prayers. At the same time, he had a mouth like a sailor and a temper to match. He had a hard time with other kids in the Sunday school setting, so Rachel and TJ kept him with them during church services. They didn't push him to behave like a Christian. Instead, they prayed for his heart to change.

They knew he was not as tough as he acted. He didn't appear to have discounted faith, but he wasn't pursuing God by any means. Sometimes Rachel felt like he was taking it all in, absorbing what it meant to be a family, to be a good man, to be a follower of God. Maybe he was weighing it with whether or not he could measure up or if he should even try.

His first summer with them Ben had attended Rachel's camp for foster children. He had been dramatically touched, softening his heart toward God and Rachel. He never fought Rachel when she sang and prayed with him after a nightmare and he joined in with the family worship around the camp fire. Sometimes he would say the most profound things about God or life. While he embraced the faith early, later he seemed to be watching, waiting to decide.

A Soft Place to Land

Rachel fiddled with her pen. How could she put into words the depth of her longing for the spiritual lives of her children? She and TJ wanted each of the kids to come into their own relationship with Jesus. It was a difficult balance to lead their children spiritually without pushing their beliefs down their throats. Some of the kids had committed their lives to Jesus when they were very young and never strayed from those early beliefs and family values. Others struggled with doubt and walked their own way before opening their hearts and lives to God. More than one had bounced around, resenting the family rules and values yet unable to ignore the love they knew God had for them. Still, none had bounced as far away as Emily. It worried Rachel.

Rachel wrote in her journal, expressing her deep hope that Ben's heart would open to God and that Emily's would soften. She laid out her prayers on paper. With her heart so heavy, her prayers were cries for God to touch the children's lives and to give her wisdom to know what to say that would bring healing and life. She prayed, wrote, read the scriptures and waited some more until a sense of peace filled her and she was comforted.

In the quietness of the morning and the stillness of her heart she heard God speak softly. "Don't be afraid to speak My truth." She jotted down what she was hearing. "Call out the light you see in them. I have my hand on them. Look for goodness and mercy and do not be discouraged. I work all things for your good and according to My good pleasure."

Rachel basked in the feeling of peace she felt in God's presence whenever she was able to quiet her own thoughts and feelings, aware of His words as they washed over her soul.

Laying her journal aside, Rachel got up from her warm spot in the big easy chair and wandered into the kitchen for another cup of coffee. TJ was standing by the window, looking out toward the pool and the gardens. He heard her come in and turned to greet her with a gentle kiss. She stood next to him gazing out the window, each lost in thought, but content to be together. TJ draped his arm around her shoulder. She felt his chest expand as he breathed deeply then exhaled slowly.

He turned from the window to look at her. She returned his gaze expectantly, but he didn't say anything.

"Did you have a good run?" she asked.

He ran several mornings a week. They both enjoyed an active outdoor lifestyle to stay in shape, but Rachel wasn't a runner. She preferred tennis, horseback riding or hiking with the boys. TJ said he ran to keep up with the kids and grandkids. He joked about getting old and slow. Rachel was sure she was becoming older and slower, but not TJ. Even with a few added pounds he was strong and fit. They loved good food with family and friends, but luckily for them, they were able to keep busy enough to compensate.

"Yep. It was good. Didn't go too far today, but got some time to kind of, you know, talk things over with God." He smiled at her. "Did you get some quiet time? I noticed you beat me out of bed this morning."

Rachel nodded. Each of them used to try to be up first. The rule was the last one out of the bed had to make it. It was a game TJ usually won during the week since he needed to check on things on the farm. They were both morning people. But TJ was also a night owl. It was more difficult for Rachel to burn the candle on both ends. She compensated by staying in bed a little longer when she could.

They moved out to the patio with their coffee, enjoying the start of a warmer-than-usual September Saturday. TJ told her more details from the night before, how he had been instantly angry at Emily and her friends when they came in with their beer bottles. He said finding out Bill and Emily were hooking up was the clincher.

"I know she is making her own choices, but I can't believe she could even like a guy like that Bill character!" He shook his head. "It was a good thing Mike was there. I would have probably just thrown Bill off the property." His eyes twinkled. "Guess I'm as hot-headed as ever about some things."

Rachel assured him any father would feel the same way.

Next, TJ brought up Ben and the incident after the game. He wondered out loud if his impatience with Emily and Bill was first ignited by the frustration he felt about Ben's attitude. Each situation was different, but TJ wanted to fix whatever was going on. It was difficult for him when he really didn't know what to do. He felt out of control when the kids simply shut down any solutions. TJ chewed on his lower lip, looking sideways at Rachel as if to judge her reaction to what he was telling her.

She nodded. She did get it. "I know. I was praying for them this morning. It is hard when you can't make them believe or make them go the way you think they should."

"The way you *know* they should," TJ corrected. "I have been where Ben is with that sullen, seething anger, and I sure as hell have been where Emily is." Rachel agreed and put her hand on his. He enfolded it and smiled at her. "But this morning as I was running and thinking about Ben and his anger I was also thinking about Emily's anger toward God. It seemed God was telling me to relax. He reminded me He's got our kids in His hands."

"Especially Ben," Rachel murmured.

"Yes, especially Ben. And of course, all of them. In spite of me, Babe. That's for sure."

"Yeah. I felt the same thing this morning. I know He's got this. I guess I just wish I knew better how to help them through everything. You know what I mean?"

TJ turned toward her and took both her hands in his. He looked earnestly into her face, locking his eyes on hers. "Oh, Babe. You always know what to do. If I could be half the parent you are—" He shook his head. "I just pray I won't get in the way, you know, mess them up from knowing God's heart as a Father to them."

"Want to pray right now?" Rachel asked.

TJ laughed. "I was just going to ask you the same thing."

"Well, you know, great minds—"

They bowed their heads and prayed, holding hands and joined in heart. They were simple prayers for love, grace and mercy as they parented their children, as they guided young lives searching for peace and truth. They prayed their kids would hunger for God and learn to trust Him above their own ideas and the wisdom of this world. They prayed for their adult children who were now parents themselves to lead their own young ones to the Father.

It dawned on Rachel they were praying not only for the

here-and-now, but for the next generation and the next. Rachel realized once again it truly was kingdom work to build bridges in their family that would lead their children and grandchildren to Jesus. She was thankful for the heritage of grace and mercy God was giving them to pass on.

CHAPTER 9
Only Human

Later in the day Emily came back to the house. She was sober, but not as humble as Rachel had hoped. Emily was never one to avoid a discussion and she approached Rachel immediately. The conversation wasn't wonderful, nor was it enjoyable, but it did provide an opportunity to hear Emily's point of view.

Emily was still angry at TJ and how wrongly she felt he had treated her friends. The more Emily ranted, the more certain Rachel was TJ had been right in taking a hard line with her. Maybe he hadn't handled it with all the finesse Rachel might have, but Emily was beyond reasoning. She was unwilling to show any remorse for her own actions. In light of Emily's current choices, TJ's firm stance seemed more than appropriate.

Rachel interrupted Emily's tirade. "Emily, how could you not have known after all this time and all the talks you have had with your dad that the situation was going to turn out exactly as it did?"

Emily shrugged defiantly.

"Come on, Emily." Rachel felt annoyed. "You know it would have been the same at Uncle Mike's and it would have been the same if it had been just me here."

Emily stood her ground. "Mom, I just don't think it is fair that everyone is expected to live the way you want them to. If they aren't perfect or whatever they can't even come over."

"Really, Em? They can't be around us?" Rachel held her daughter's gaze. "You know that isn't true."

"Isn't it?" Emily stood up, getting more agitated. "Mom, you think you are so open-minded, but seriously, you guys are so uptight about stuff!" Emily threw her hands in the air. "Ugh! Mom! You can't expect everyone to live by the same rules as you and Dad." Emily ended with a mutter about how no one lived the way they did. Rachel was pretty sure she heard Emily say something about the dark ages.

Rachel thoughtfully considered her words. She wondered if there was anything she could say in this moment that would make a difference. She didn't want the conversation to end with them both upset. If Emily left angry it was likely to be a long time before she came home again.

She didn't care that they didn't agree, but she wanted Emily to be calm enough to realize that no matter what their differences she could always come home. Grace and

Chapter 9: Only Human

boundaries—both were God's ways, but how could she help their children see both in their home? She pondered this while Emily continued to rant about rules and being told her choices were not acceptable.

It came to Rachel that Emily's anger might be masking guilt and perhaps shame. Rachel put her hand up to stop her.

"Em, Honey, what is this really about?" She looked at her daughter with compassion, but she spoke quietly and firmly. "You girls have all grown up knowing what is allowed here. Is this really about the rules?"

Emily stopped talking for a moment. Rachel thought she saw something of the truth go across her face.

Rachel continued. "I'm wondering if maybe you are angry because you are ashamed about your behavior. Or maybe you feel out of control with how much you are drinking and partying."

Emily dropped her head, picking at her fingernail. Rachel watched her silently for a moment. She touched Emily's arm.

"Do you need help?"

Emily didn't look up. She let Rachel stay close. Rachel waited. Finally, Emily looked straight at her.

"No. I've got this, Mom. Just because I drink, sometimes

too much I'll admit, doesn't mean I have a problem." She faltered a moment then she became indignant again. "No, I don't have a problem. Maybe you and Dad have a problem with anybody having a good time." She was back in her anger. She moved away from Rachel. "You know what? I don't want to talk about this anymore. I get it. If I can't be perfect I just won't come over."

Rachel's heart ached. She reached out to touch Emily, but Emily jerked away. Rachel's hand dropped. Again she sought to choose just the right words.

"Oh, Em. I'm just worried about you." Empathy engulfed Rachel as she tried to initiate a truce. "We don't see you much these days and I don't want to spend the time we have fighting. I miss you and I am worried about you. You are truly an amazing young woman and artist. I just don't want to see you throw away everything you once believed in. It is hard to watch that happen. Maybe you can't see how close you are to heading into disaster. What kind of parents would we be if we did not warn you? We want you to pursue your dreams, but Em, don't get lost seeking after lesser things."

Rachel fought tears. "I know you think we are overreacting. I hear you saying you have control of your drinking, and your life, but you might be the only one who actually believes it. I wish you could see what we—your family, who love you tons, by the way—see. Then you might understand."

Chapter 9: Only Human

Emily paused. Her face softened. She looked ready to give in. Rachel moved toward her again. But then Emily stiffened. Her eyes grew hard and dark.

"I know you love me. But you don't understand me. I'm fine! And I am doing better than anyone else I know who is in this business. I know I shouldn't have been drinking here, and I'm even willing to say I am sorry for that. As far as all the rest, I still think you and Dad should apologize to Bill for taking his keys, and for being so stubborn. You need to realize that I am grown up and I can do whatever the hell I want. I just won't do it around you."

Rachel bit hard on the side of her mouth to keep from replying. She took a deep breath and slowly exhaled. Emily looked at her with defiance, daring her to contradict her. But Rachel sadly shook her head.

"You're right, Emily. You can live however you want. You can choose to ignore wisdom and advice. You can compare yourself to everyone around you and feel pretty good about your choices. And you might even fit in really well with everyone else. Our hope for you, for your sisters and brothers, for your nieces and nephews, is not to merely fit in or be a little more moral than the next person. Our hope for you is a life of integrity, of honor, a life pleasing to God. What that looks like, how you live that out, is yours to discover. But it is our place as parents, as family, to encourage you in any way we can to live it out. If it means it is hard for you to be around because it makes you feel bad, then I guess it is what it is." Rachel folded her arms with finality.

Emily didn't meet Rachel's eye. "Okay, I get it." And the conversation was over.

They didn't talk about it again during the weekend. Emily spent a little time with her brothers, hung out with Mary in the cottage after dinner and by Sunday morning was getting ready for her next concert. Then she was gone.

Rachel wished she could feel better about Emily. But the truth was, the distance between them seemed to grow with each road trip. And Rachel worried.

CHAPTER 10
Two Lanes of Freedom

The first two months of school were all about getting into a routine with homework, afterschool practices, football games and cross country meets. The schedule was consuming and at times Rachel felt overwhelmed. She went through this every fall. The girls had been just as active in sports during their junior high and senior high school years, and Rachel had been just as besieged trying to keep up.

When she had been a single mom she had also worked fulltime as a therapist running the non-profit center Naomi now directed. Then marrying and bringing the boys into their family had been her fulltime job. For TJ as well. Both TJ and Rachel had streamlined their activities, cutting back on work outside the home. Even now, Rick and Ben required a high level of support and supervision. Thankfully, Rachel had restricted her working to a small amount of equine-assisted psychotherapy at the farm, mostly with families and children from Hope Enterprises programs. She and TJ made sure at least one of them was always available to provide the level of care the boys needed. It was a juggling act for sure.

Their family enjoyed keeping busy. TJ no longer

managed Hope Enterprises, but he continued to be involved with development of new ideas. He had been an active part of coaching or helping with the kids' sports since his girls had played T-ball. Rachel and TJ led a support group for adoptive parents throughout the year. They had offers on the table to speak about adoption. Rachel was often asked to lead conferences or provide workshops on helping kids heal from trauma. TJ still dabbled in music and was often asked to sing at events, and he occasionally recorded with other artists. They didn't travel far from home very often because in the midst of it all Rachel and TJ did their best to keep routines stable for the boys and provide the structure they craved.

This fall things seemed to be going fairly well. Ben was struggling to keep up with school and football, but there hadn't been any negative reports from the school. Ricky was his usual happy, easy-going self as he managed to juggle classes with cross country and develop socially. Rachel and TJ felt confident Ben and Ricky were settling down and adjusting to Heritage.

They were cautiously optimistic. After years of difficulties with the boys at school and at home, Rachel was never certain of what normalcy really looked like. At times she and TJ endured months of being at the school almost every day with either Rick or Ben or hours at home of holding

Chapter 10: Two Lanes of Freedom

one or the other, sitting with them or walking while they ranted, cried, or raged. In different ways, the boys struggled to accept the love and safety of their new home. Parenting children with a history of trauma was challenging and many times stretched them to their limits.

It was "back to school" night at Heritage and Rachel was meeting TJ so they could design a plan for each getting all the classrooms. Though it was the boys' first year at Heritage, the staff was familiar with Ben's and Ricky's history and the Keytons were one of the better-known families there because of TJ's fame and their long history with the school. Still, Rachel did not feel as involved in this setting as she had at the boys' previous schools. She considered that with TJ's helping with the sporting programs and his financial contributions to the school, perhaps less would be required of her here.

As Rachel sped toward the school, she wondered how in the world she and TJ had done these back-to-school nights with six kids. How she had done it for seven years as a single parent was beyond her. She already dreaded rushing from classroom to classroom. She would barely see TJ as they each went different ways. If she found him before it started she might be able to say a "See ya later," before the mad dash.

TJ was already at the school. He had stayed after football

for a meeting with the coach. Mary had picked up the boys and taken them home while Rachel made dinner. She'd eaten with them before getting ready to leave. Ben needed her help with his social history homework. Tired from his own day and stressed because he had waited until the last minute to do it, his frustration and anger were surfacing quickly. Rachel was able to keep him from erupting by showing him several small steps to the project and giving him some needed materials. She had to rely on Mary to help him through the first few steps so he would be calm enough to finish the task. Now she was hurrying, hating to be late.

Thankfully, once inside the building, TJ was easy to spot. He was standing next to the principal. He caught her eye and waved her over, then teasingly pointed at his watch. She gave him her best "don't go there" look and was relieved to see he had the schedules for the night. Ben and Rick were supposed to have brought them home, but of course, neither had been able to find them when she asked for them.

"Oh good, you've got them!" she greeted her husband. A few other parents crowded in to speak with Principal Harper, so she and TJ stepped aside to survey the papers.

"How do you want to do this? Do you want me to take one and you take the other?"

Rachel scanned the schedules and noted the teachers she

Chapter 10: Two Lanes of Freedom

already knew. Feeling tired and dreading trying to cover the list, she lost all interest in being in separate classrooms all evening.

"You know, Babe, we don't have to go to all of these. What would you think about going together and hitting the classrooms we most need to cover?"

TJ shrugged in his nonchalant manner.

Rachel pressed on, feeling somehow she had to convince him. "We know the teachers. We met with most of them before school started."

"Hey, I am with you." TJ put up his hands. "I don't want to scurry around going in different directions either. Haven't we been doing that for twelve years now? I'm game. Let's go!"

Rachel looked up at his smiling face. He winked at her and put his arm around her shoulders. They skimmed the two schedules.

"Great. So let's do these then." Rachel pointed to the classes she thought they most needed to visit. The bell rang, signaling for the parents to move. Rachel laughed at how refreshed she suddenly felt. She would get to be with TJ after all.

TJ took her hand as they elbowed down the hallway, trying

not to be tardy to the first session. "Gotta love back-to-school night," he called over his shoulder. "Makes me feel like I'm in high school again every time." He chuckled softly, slowed his pace, leaning toward her ear, and whispered, "Want to go out with me?"

Rachel grinned and nodded. "You know, you did actually ask me that before, just like this, except over the phone, remember?"

"Yeah, I remember. I was really nervous. Felt just like a teenager."

They slipped into seats at the back of the science room while the instructor distributed hand-outs. TJ whispered, "We should have date night more often. This is really fun."

Rachel laughed silently and shook her head at him. "Shh. Silly cowboy. There is no way you are getting off that easy. If this is a date night, you better be thinking of what else you can do."

"Buy you lunch at the cafeteria? Carry your books? Help you—"

Rachel was just about to laugh when the teacher shot them a look. She raised an eyebrow and nudged TJ to be quiet.

"Stop trying to get me in trouble," she whispered in a feigned stern voice. She gazed raptly at the front of the room,

Chapter 10: Two Lanes of Freedom

pretending to be interested in what the teacher was saying. TJ took her snub as an invitation to try harder to get her attention. Rachel did her best to keep her eyes forward, but she was more aware of him than anything else. She could hear his pen scratching on the back of the handout. She wondered if he was seriously taking notes. She doubted it. He was a major distraction. She tried using her peripheral vision to see what he was up to. She didn't want the teacher to know she wasn't paying attention. She'd given up listening, but did her best to pretend she was. TJ rustled the paper and fidgeted in his chair. Rachel was getting a good idea what he must have been like in school.

As the teacher explained the parental access code to the school site, TJ inched his desk closer to Rachel's. It took all her self-control to stifle a giggle when she realized he was right beside her. TJ slipped a note onto her desk. She unfolded it as quietly as she could and hoped no one else was watching them.

It read: *Hey, girl. Want to sneak out after class? Check yes or no.*

Rachel quickly jotted, *Maybe*, and put a check by it. She slipped the note back to him.

She sneaked a glance at him to see his reaction. He winked at her, added to the note then handed it back. *If we were in high school together, there is no way I could sit this close to you and concentrate on science. Let's get lost for a bit.*

Rachel was sure she was blushing. She put her hand on her cheek, trying to regain her composure, but inside she felt warm and tingly. She gave the note back to him with her approval to abort all plans of being responsible parents. By that time the session was ending and the teacher dismissed them.

With a playful grin, TJ hurried her out of the room without so much as a word to the instructor or other parents. She followed him into the hall, now filled with adults trying to find their way to their next stop.

Once away from the science room, TJ looked at her with a big grin on his face. She pulled his head down for a kiss.

"Hey, no PDA!" A man chortled as he passed them. It was one of the fathers Rachel recognized from football practice. He and TJ exchanged greetings as they resumed their way down the hall and toward the side door out to the parking lot.

"You all leaving?" This time it was the principal, the man TJ had been talking to earlier.

"Damn," TJ muttered under his breath. To Marc Harper, he said, "Yeah, something came up and we gotta go. See ya tomorrow." TJ grabbed Rachel's hand as she was giving a

Chapter 10: Two Lanes of Freedom

short wave goodbye. She was having a tough time trying not to look too happy about leaving. They rushed out the door and dashed to TJ's jeep. He deftly opened the door for her.

"Get in quick, Babe, before someone else comes and tries to talk to us." She nimbly jumped in as he shut the door and ran to the other side. They were both breathing hard and laughing as he started the engine. "Reminds me of escaping from fans, but I think I'm a bit rusty."

"I can't believe we just did that." Rachel laughed. "Heritage is small enough, you know, they're gonna know we weren't there." She punched his arm playfully. "You're a bad influence."

"Me? I was just passing notes. You're the one that was all over me like white on rice in the hallway back there."

"White on rice? Whatever." She put her hand over his on the gear shaft. "So where are you taking me?"

"I don't know. As far as I got in my planning was the escape." They laughed. "Rache, seriously, we have got to get more time for stuff like this. I miss you, girl."

"Hmmm. I think so, too. School time is just so full of responsibilities for us. Between keeping the kids on schedule, and sports, with the boys in high school, autumn is one big have- to-do list."

TJ agreed. But she knew the things they had to do were a big part of what they wanted to do. It was crazy hectic, but they both loved it. Rachel leaned back and relaxed her shoulders.

They weren't saying much. TJ turned on the radio. She loved it when he sang along as he drove. This was what she wanted. His rich voice calming every part of her mind and soul. She closed her eyes. She was content.

TJ stopped singing. "Hey, don't fall asleep on me. I'll turn this Jeep right around and take you back to algebra class! I'm not used to putting people to sleep, you know."

"I'm not sleeping. Just enjoying going nowhere and listening to you sing." Rachel suddenly sat up in the seat. "Oh wait, turn it up. It's Emily!"

"Now you're awake!" TJ cranked the volume.

When the song ended, Rachel gravely asked, "TJ, how do you think she's doing?"

He didn't answer right away. Rachel watched him carefully weighing his reply. Finally, he said he thought Emily was doing great. But something in his hesitation and the way he chewed his bottom lip caused Rachel to doubt his words.

"Really?"

Chapter 10: *Two Lanes of Freedom*

"Sure, Babe. Emily is going to be great." He gave her a reassuring smile.

"I don't mean about her music. How is she *doing* doing?"

Again, he was slow to answer. Rubbing his chin, he appeared to be contemplating what to say.

"Do you really want to talk about that now? Tonight?" He finally asked.

"I don't know. Well, yeah, I guess I do. When else can we talk about it without other ears listening in? What is it? Are you worried about her? I know I am."

"Okay." He sighed. "Well, I think Emily has a good head on her shoulders despite her recent choices." He stole a glance at her. "I can't explain how heady it is when you start to have real success in this business, Rachel. But yeah, I believe in her and I think she'll come back around before too long." His voice was more somber than his promising words. Rachel leaned forward to search his face. She saw worry in his eyes.

"I hope you're right," she said. She felt TJ tense.

"What's that supposed to mean?" he asked curtly.

"Nothing. I just hope you're right that she is going to pass through this phase and find stability."

"Well, there are no guarantees for any of our kids, Rachel." His voice had an edge to it. "Just because she is in the music business doesn't mean she wouldn't have struggled if she had done something else."

Rachel felt his defensiveness. She bristled even though she had been relaxed just moments before, instantly irritated at the harshness in his tone. She didn't take time to figure out what had changed in their conversation or why she was feeling annoyed herself. She immediately reacted.

"Well, duh, TJ. It's not like I expect my kids to be totally perfect and not make mistakes. It's not like we haven't been through difficulties with each one of them. Look at Gracie and what we went through with her. But she's doing great now. What about the challenges with Hope her first year of college and how depressed she was? And Naomi, not knowing what she wanted to do? Shoot, Ben and Ricky are all about their issues. They have all had their moments. Geez, TJ, I only asked you about Emily because you understand what is going on with her right now better than I do."

"So then are you saying it is my fault?" His voice was louder than necessary. "It's my fault she is where she is?"

Rachel couldn't believe he was going there. She gave him a peeved look, but he kept going.

"Are you saying I am not doing enough for her?"

Chapter 10: *Two Lanes of Freedom*

Rachel shook her head but TJ ignored her.

"It sounds like you think I did more for the other kids. What, is it because she isn't mine?" He pulled the Jeep over and slammed it into park. He gave her a hard stare. "You don't think I am doing everything I can to help your kids, too? Is that it?"

"What? TJ. No, of course not." Rachel felt angry and bitter at his accusation. She didn't offer any soothing words because of her own rising defensiveness.

"Well, what is it then?" His tone demanded a response. "I worry about her just like I do all our kids."

"I know that, TJ." Rachel swallowed hard. She hadn't seen him get argumentative like this in a long time. "TJ, what are you being so defensive about? When have I ever said you would only take care of your kids? I don't even think of the kids as yours or mine." Rachel could feel her blood coursing through her as she struggled to keep her voice even. Even trying to relax, Rachel felt frustrated. His jaw was set. He seemed determined to take whatever she said the wrong way. She waited for him to respond.

"It just sounds like you're still mad I got her into the music business, that's all." He looked straight ahead at the road. Rachel wanted to read his face. She was already feeling sorry getting so provoked so quickly. Maybe he felt sorry, too.

"No, I didn't mean that at all." She softened her voice. "I just wanted some reassurance from you that Emily is going to be okay."

"Well, how am I supposed to know that?" His irritation was not waning.

Rachel regretted the way the conversation had turned. She wanted to do something to get back to the place where they were before Emily's song. She hated the tension in the Jeep. They didn't often argue. And even when they did disagree there wasn't usually this kind of edginess in their exchanges. Rachel could feel his touchiness with everything she said. She tried to focus on what he might really be feeling rather than what he was saying. The truth was, she was struggling to clear her own thoughts as she fought to keep from being offended by his attitude. She decided to stick to explaining her intentions rather than trying to mitigate his mood.

"I don't know, Babe." She chose her words carefully. "I guess I asked you how she was doing so that you would ease my mind. I needed to hear you say she is going to be okay."

Rachel thought over TJ's initial response. "You did try to reassure me, I know, but I think in my worrying I just wanted you to tell me I had nothing to fret about."

Chapter 10: Two Lanes of Freedom

Heavy silence filled the Jeep.

Finally Rachel put her hand on his arm. "I don't know why this conversation is going all wrong." TJ rubbed his chin and looked sideways at her. She kept her hand on his arm and willed herself to listen and not react.

He exhaled noisily. "It just feels like whenever you ask me about Emily it's like you are blaming me for getting her into the business. Then I think I should apologize to you for encouraging her in that direction. It seems like you think I did the wrong thing by her, even though she is going to be great."

Rachel shook her head. A long time ago, they had argued about Emily going to college before starting a music career. They disagreed about when or how much TJ should help her get on her way. They had both been apprehensive for her and what the road would be like. For a while even after she was out of school and playing music she was struggling so much to make it they worried together about how she was surviving and about how to help her. They hadn't talked much about what would happen when Emily did succeed.

TJ and Tina were pulling as many strings as they could without Emily feeling she was getting handouts. As Rachel thought about the last few years she couldn't remember once saying or thinking the music business was somehow wrong for Emily. She certainly didn't blame TJ for Emily's choices.

Rachel knew once Emily decided to be a singer no one was going to stop her. She had been glad Emily had TJ and Tina to help her through the maze of getting a manager and finding a producer she could trust. Rachel thought about the comfort she felt knowing TJ had his eye and other eyes looking out for Emily. She tried to convey this to TJ. She told him again she didn't fault him at all for helping her.

TJ turned and faced her. "Really, Rache?"

She nodded.

His voice softened. "I do worry about her, too, because, you know, I have been on the wild side of this business and I know how easy it is to flow with it. It was a lot harder than anyone could imagine to live with success and be godly and principled. I never wanted any of my kids to walk that path. Then I met you, and your daughter was the one out of all the kids who decided to go into country music. I just feel like maybe if she hadn't been so excited about it from me and Tina you wouldn't be so worried about her." He looked down at his hands and fiddled with his ring.

"TJ," Rachel said softly and waited until he looked up. She put her hand on his. "Maybe you blame yourself. But I'm not blaming you. You're right, all of our kids have had their battles and there will be more ahead, I am sure. You have to know, Babe, that Emily wanted to be a superstar long before she met you. She made up her mind. I think it was the first time we ever went to a Katrina Metcafe concert when she was seven years old."

It was quiet and Rachel felt the tension in the Jeep starting to ease. In her mind she went over how quickly the argument had arisen. She saw it as an indication of how tired and stressed they were. TJ getting defensive so quickly was rare. Rachel wondered about the pressure he was under.

"Humph." TJ broke the silence. "I guess it's Tina's fault then." His voice was dead serious, but his eyes held the familiar twinkle he always got when joking around. Then he snickered. "Come to think of it, it was her fault I even met you and your girls in the first place."

"Tina's fault!" They said it simultaneously, laughing.

"You owe me a drink, mister, for that jinx," Rachel said.

TJ agreed. Then he came up with a better idea. He moved his seat back from the steering wheel and reached for her. Rachel leaned toward him and they kissed the best they could with the gear shift and bucket seats separating them. For comfort's sake, they pulled apart sooner than they wanted to.

"Damn, this used to be easier, too," TJ grumbled. "I haven't gotten lucky in a vehicle in a long time."

"You won't tonight either." Rachel joked. "We would probably both end up at the chiropractor's or worse."

TJ agreed on that one. He told her he was sorry for being so quick to get angry.

"Guess we both feel the strain of another school year," she replied.

"Well, I think this thing with Emily has been bugging me for a while. I feel responsible for her. I think I feel a little guilty, too, about how much fun it is having a kid doing all this great stuff. But then I think about all the pitfalls and I feel kinda guilty about wanting her to have success. I want her to make it big and at the same time I want her to stay young and innocent." He shook his head, and rubbed his jaw. "I know I need to trust God for her well-being and I'm not. That's probably why I was so hard on her when she brought those guys over. I want her to get her act together so I don't feel guilty. I guess I convinced myself you were blaming me, too."

Rachel assured him she wrestled with the same feelings.

"Watching our kids thrash about is tough. I sure don't handle it the best. Sorry, Babe, for being so defensive."

He smiled at her warmly. "Rache, honestly sometimes I think being a parent is a constant sense of falling. When I fail

Chapter 10: Two Lanes of Freedom

I am so glad you are here to pick me up, brush me off and send me back in the game." He gave a short laugh.

Rachel chuckled too. It was exactly how she felt about life sometimes—falling down, making mistakes, being forgiven and loved, and set back on the path. Family was a soft place to land, but falling was still hard.

TJ turned the Jeep back toward the school. Rachel stroked the back of his hand as she thought about falling and family. She recognized how important he was to her and to their kids. "Babe, would you believe me if I said you were the best thing that ever happened to me, to my girls? I know it sounds sappy, but really, I am so thankful for you."

"Thanks, Darlin.'" He tipped his imaginary hat to her and winked. "Sure you aren't just getting used to me?"

"Well, there is that."

CHAPTER 11
From Ben's Journal

I don't know where I started going wrong, but I can't for the life of me keep it together. I am just so pissed off all the time. Even when I am trying to make good choices and do the right thing I keep messing up. I hate it. I thought I was past all this crap.

When I was a little kid I used to fight all the time. I fought at school with other kids all the time. Once I moved in here, then I fought a lot with my family, especially my mother. It doesn't make sense, but I guess I wasn't too sure I wanted a family. Mama says it is more that I didn't know I could trust a family so I was pushing everyone away. Maybe. I just know I was really mad all the time. Even though I didn't have any birth family except for Ricky, I didn't know for sure if I would want this family. That really doesn't make sense, I know. I guess it was just too scary to let myself like them and then maybe be sent away.

Seems pretty crazy looking back now, but I would throw these huge fits where I would just scream and yell and throw stuff. I said hateful things to my mother. I didn't want anyone to be in control of me but I couldn't control myself either. Too much crap had happened to me and my brother and I guess someone had to pay for it. My parents had to prove to me I was safe and they could handle me. They would hold me close and I would fight against them, but then I just started giving up or maybe it was giving in. I stopped fighting so much but I also stopped feeling so angry. I couldn't change them and somehow that helped me trust them. I kinda settled into the family and it felt good. Mama and I talked through a lot of the stuff that happened to me and Ricky. I still have a hard time not getting angry quickly but I can usually cope with it and get myself settled before I do something stupid. Until this football season it has been getting better and it for sure hasn't been this bad. Now I am mad again all the time. And it sucks.

I don't like this feeling. I feel so mad at everyone right now. I am starting to hate my football team. Along with hating my team, my dad is just driving me crazy. I don't know why. Plus I can't concentrate on school. I really don't understand what is going on. I can't seem to get a handle on anything. I haven't told Mama and Daddy yet, but I'm not getting my school work done. I tried really hard at first to keep it all together at school and at football. I just can't.

I'm pretty sure something bad is going to happen. My parents are going to find out about my grades soon. And about football, well, I think Coach has just about had it

Chapter 11: From Ben's Journal

with me. And since all this started going south, I've had this out-of-control, angry feeling inside my chest all the time. I actually can't believe Mama hasn't said anything about it. Usually she can read me like a book. But maybe it's because things are okay at home. I mean, at home I am kind of holding it together for the most part. If I get kicked off the team for my grades or for fighting, my dad is going to be really mad at me. At least once it happens it will be over and maybe I can just chill out.

CHAPTER 12
Boys of Fall

Rachel watched TJ chew nervously on his fingernail as Coach Fischer hollered at Ben. She could tell TJ was trying to stay out of it. Kyle stood nearby, taking in the lecture with a smug look on his face. Apparently Ben had missed the tackle, making it impossible for Kyle to be in place to make the catch. The quarterback had yelled at Ben to do a better job blocking. Ben ripped off his helmet and started yelling obscenities. Kyle made a snide comment and Ben didn't hesitate to throw a punch. Unfortunately for Ben, Kyle still had on his helmet making Ben's punch much less effective than Kyle's counterattack to Ben's unprotected face.

TJ ran out to separate the boys, nose to nose in a heated exchange. Coach Fischer marched over to the boys and pushed TJ aside.

"Let me handle it, Keyton!" he called sharply.

"Oh my, Rachel thought, "this is going to get ugly." When Ben was this escalated it rarely helped for an angry adult to yell at him. Coach Fischer was clearly angry at this latest outburst. Although the exchanges between Ben and Kyle had lessened, Ben had continued to struggle with just about everyone on the team. He was quick to fight and he was getting benched more often than he was playing. Kyle was cocky and mean-spirited. But truth was, Ben's problems in getting along with others weren't limited to this one boy. What worried Rachel is how Ben's hostility was intensifying.

TJ had been trying hard to keep Ben focused on the game. He'd encouraged him to overlook the normal team teasing or razzing and concentrate on his skills. Privately, TJ had begun to voice doubts about Ben's ability to emotionally control himself. Rachel had wondered often at the wisdom of placing Ben in such an aggressive team sport. Every practice, every game, every day presented challenges for Ben to stay balanced.

The combination of such a physical game with a stressed, adrenaline-pumped adolescent who is easily over-stimulated and has deep-seated anger issues seemed to be a recipe for problems. It was a lot to expect from any young man. A lot of kids playing aggressive sports struggle with aggression in other areas. Ben seemed to be on the losing side of self-control.

Rachel sighed and shook her head. The last three games Ben had been pulled off the field. She usually saw it coming. He would miss a block or make a mistake, maybe a bad call—anything could set him off—and then he would be infuriated. Next thing she knew he would be yelling,

Chapter 12: Boys of Fall

throwing his helmet, or letting punches fly. At games, it was usually taken out on an opponent. But if a team member or a ref was nearby they might also be his target. More than once Rachel had questioned TJ if he could see it coming from the sidelines. She pointed out how clearly she could see it from the stands. It was maddening to watch.

"Maybe it is just too much for him, TJ," she said, trying again to explain Ben's inability to regulate so many opposing emotions. They had just witnessed a particularly bad game, although games-gone-bad were becoming the norm. If Ben weren't such a good player no one would put up with his unrelenting attitude.

"Do you want me to tell him he can't play?" TJ responded testily. Ben had been benched twice for unnecessary roughness. Rachel had brought up Ben's consistent failure to channel his anger. "He loves the game, Rache. I love watching him play. Don't you think we are working through it? Maybe it is good for him to have this constant challenge."

"Maybe." She was unconvinced. She, too, loved watching him play—when he was playing and not losing it out on the field. As soon as his frustration started to kick in she could feel the tension all over her. Most games, her stomach hurt. She felt edgy and nervous watching him unravel. And hearing the comments from other parents was tough on her. They joked about beating the attitude out of him if he were their kid. Rachel would square her shoulders and scoot a little closer to Tina, trying not to let it—any of it—get to her.

Many people had opinions about what they would do if Ben were their child, but none of them had raised a child with attachment issues. It took more than traditional parenting to reach kids who were from hard places like her boys had come from. Rachel was used to stares from "you shoulders," especially when the boys had been younger. She knew those closest to her realized how much Ben had overcome. She found solidarity in knowing their family understood how very difficult all this was for him.

At games, Rachel stayed close to Beth or Tina. When things got tense she gripped their hands and prayed silently. Last Friday night Ben had been put back in the game after two near-fights. It was the end of the fourth quarter and she could see Coach Fischer was trying to give Ben a chance to end the game well. One parent stood up and yelled, "Don't put that kid back in there. Little brat doesn't know how to do anything but fight."

"Shut-up!" Rachel leaped from her seat and turned to glare at the man.

"Why don't you make him?" the woman next to him dared her.

Rachel stared angrily at both of them.

Chapter 12: Boys of Fall

Beth took her arm and pulled to encourage her to sit down. "Mom," she warned between gritted teeth.

Tears smarted Rachel's eyes. She wasn't prone to yell at refs, coaches or anyone. Rarely did she even comment on bad calls. But the man's comment was more than she could take, especially as she was already keenly aware of Ben unraveling on the field. It had become so difficult to watch him struggle out there, knowing he was completely frustrated, and yet unable to pull himself together.

She could see how it looked to the others watching, but her emotions were pulled between sadness and concern. It was so difficult to stand by, unable to do anything. She knew Ben was wrong. She didn't want him fighting with other kids. But she also knew how hard he was trying and she wished others could see it, too.

"I know, Beth," Rachel whispered to her daughter. She felt her face hot with embarrassment. She heard a few snickers and comments behind her, but she kept her back stiff and her face forward until the end of the game. She wanted to say something to the parents—something about acknowledging she wasn't condoning Ben's behavior, but also pointing out how hard the boys worked and they didn't deserve the rude comments of parents who should concentrate on encouraging rather than destroying them.

Rachel was beginning to dread games. Today, with Ben being chewed out at practice, Rachel felt the sinking feeling she'd experienced every game day the past few weeks. She wrapped her coat and scarf more tightly around her. It was the end of October and the wind bit cruelly even though the sun warmed the field. Rachel couldn't watch. It hurt too much. Her mother's heart was not cut out for the words exchanged between coaches and players, and sometimes dads and sons.

Her approach was softer. TJ was a good dad, kind and understanding, but he was also firm and demanding at times. Rachel had never been a yeller, and neither she nor TJ were prone to losing their tempers with any of their kids. They worked hard to provide structure and yet grace. But there were times all the kids, especially the boys, needed the strength of men like TJ and Coach Fischer. She just couldn't watch it.

So instead, she studied TJ. He had turned his shoulder away from the scene, but he was listening. Ben was certainly getting an earful. TJ glanced up and saw Rachel watching him. He shook his head slightly. Rachel knew it was hard on him, too. He didn't think it was going very well, that much was clear. TJ walked back to the other players finishing up their drills. He clapped the shoulders of the first guys on their way to the showers.

Rachel couldn't hear much of what was being said, but

Chapter 12: Boys of Fall

from what she could see, Coach Fischer was at the end of his patience. As a parting shot, she heard the coach yell for Ben to get his act together and be a team player. Rachel knew Ben was running out of chances with the frustrated coach. To the man's credit, he had given Ben more opportunities than he would any other kid. It had to be discouraging for him and the team that Ben's problems seemed to be getting worse. After weeks of extra drills for losing his temper, many apologies and being benched over and over, Ben still could not regulate his temper. He was better about not blaming everyone else and better at saying he was sorry, but other than that, it was hard to see if he was actually more frustrated or just cared less about stifling it.

Ben said something back to the coach that Rachel was unable to hear. Whatever it was, Coach Fischer was livid. He turned back toward Ben and stepped in closer. Rachel instinctively leaned in a little, too.

"Do you want to get kicked off this team, Son?" Fischer's face was red with anger. "Is that it?"

Ben stood his ground where other kids would have cowered. He looked angry and defiant.

The coach continued, "You're a damn good player, but you have got to pull yourself together."

Ben didn't move. His body was tense. Rachel couldn't see

his face, but from his tightly fisted hands and stiff stance she was sure his eyes were hard. He used anger to keep everyone away, but when it was thrown back at him he tended to shut down.

The coach was rarely confrontational to the players. He was hard-nosed with high expectations, but usually stayed in control. TJ moved over and stood next Ben.

Ben broke his stare-down with the coach and glanced at TJ. Rachel held her breath. She prayed as she was sure TJ was, too. She silently begged Ben to relax. Finally, Ben looked down at his hands. Rachel saw him purposefully unclench his fists. He looked again at his dad. He said something, too soft for Rachel to hear, but TJ dropped his head and Coach Fischer backed off. Ben remained sullen and disengaged as the coach placed his hand on his shoulder.

"Son, you are going to have to figure that one out," Rachel heard the coach say.

A few more words were exchanged before Ben was dismissed and took off toward the locker room. Ricky was running toward Ben from the far side of the track. Rachel lingered, watching Ricky next to Ben. He was talking a mile a minute about something. He didn't seem to mind that Ben wasn't talking at all. He made it easy for Ben to just be lost in his own thoughts.

TJ stood talking to Coach Fischer. Rachel decided against joining the discussion. Instead, she walked slowly behind her sons.

CHAPTER 13
From Ricky's Journal

Here's the thing—I know my brother better than anyone. Maybe even better than he knows himself. I could have told my parents he was lying and I sure could have told them he was afraid to tell them he really doesn't want to play football anymore. So that's why a few weeks ago when he really started fighting with the guys on the team more and being even more surly than usual I knew things were getting worse for him.

I told him he should talk to Daddy about it, but he pretty much told me to mind my own business. I got mad at him and told him he was my business, but I also told him I wouldn't tell our parents. Then Ben told me about his grades and how scared he was of letting everyone—well mostly Daddy—down.

Ben will talk to me, but sometimes it takes a while to break through his anger. My dad and Ben have always connected. And after listening to Ben tell me how worried he was that Daddy would hate him for failing at football I realized how much of their bond was through sports. Ben wants Daddy to be proud of him. I know deep down my brother is totally scared of disappointing our father. And with Ben, whatever he is afraid of, he fights. No wonder he has been so angry at the football team and really at Daddy.

I tried to convince Ben that Daddy would be okay with it all if he was honest and really talked to him. But Ben couldn't see that. So I promised I wouldn't say anything. Ben has always had my back. He is my protector and there is no way I would hurt him by telling on him. But on the other hand, I hate all the tension in our house. I hope no one asks me what I think about football and my brother's problems out on the field. I won't lie about it, but so far no one has asked me. Which is pretty funny since Ben and I are so close.

CHAPTER 14
Heart to Heart

After the confrontation at football practice, TJ and Ben were unusually quiet during dinner. Rachel searched their faces hoping to catch the eye of either one. Ricky chatted about school, his video game, what he wanted to do next weekend. Rachel tried to follow his flow of conversation, but it was tough to keep up. When there was tension, Rick often talked more. She knew he was filling up the silence, and tonight she let him.

She figured Ben would talk when he was ready. But the troubled look on TJ's face made her uneasy. Rick tried to connect with his dad a few times during their meal, but TJ was distant and distracted.

After Ricky asked him about plans for Halloween TJ said, "I'm sorry Son. I got some things on my mind and I wasn't listening."

Rick frowned a little, but then he turned his questions and chatter to Ben. Ben was not any more engaged. He shrugged every once in a while and finally asked to be excused from the table. Rachel reminded him about getting his homework done. "Yes, Ma'am," he mumbled, as he rinsed his plate and put his dirty dishes in the dishwasher.

Rachel caught TJ watching him, his face full of concern. Ricky quickly asked if he could go with Ben and started up from the table. "No." TJ put his hand on Rick's arm. "First you need to take care of your business here." He pointed to his dinner plate. "And I think you need to just give your brother a little space right now."

Rick groaned and sank back into his chair. "What's up with you all anyway?" he asked. "It's not like anything new is going on. Ben always gets into fights. Seems like you just keep thinking it will be different and then you all get upset when you don't see any change. How's it supposed to change when nothing else changes?"

TJ grunted and shook his head. He looked over at Rachel. The kid had a point. Rachel smiled slightly as TJ said, "Yeah, I guess you're right, Ricky." TJ turned to Rachel, "Maybe the stuff we are trying isn't working. But I'm not sure what we can do right now, except ride it out."

Rachel reached over and patted Rick's arm. She didn't want him to worry. She got up and said lightly, "Come on men. Help me clear these dishes."

Never one to be discouraged for long, Ricky was already up and putting things in the sink. He finished quickly and Rachel reminded him about getting his clothes out of the dryer, folding them and taking them up to his room. Grumbling a little, he left the kitchen.

Chapter 14: *Heart to Heart*

TJ came over to the sink where Rachel was rinsing dishes. He leaned against the counter facing her. She paused and studied his face. Something more than Ben fighting was weighing on him. She waited for him to tell her.

"He told the coach he wants to quit," he said, fiddling with his ring. Rachel could feel TJ's struggle beyond words. It was almost as though it was hurting him to see Ben so ready to give up. Maybe all of it played on his own sense of powerlessness because he couldn't fix it or make Ben do better.

"Oh, TJ. He said that?"

TJ nodded thoughtfully but did not offer any further information.

Rachel kept her eyes on his face, wishing she could say something that would help. There was sometimes a hurt in Ricky that touched Rachel deeply, like a reminder of a lingering pain she was familiar with. She saw this same depth of emotion now in TJ about Ben. There was something is Ben's actions and anger that often triggered a deep pain in TJ. In this way, these boys were more like her and TJ than their biological children. When she felt these raw emotions touch her and TJ like this Rachel knew the boys were truly their soul children. She and TJ had often talked about how they felt related to the boys in their struggles in the same way they saw themselves in their biological children. Rachel was sure TJ was having one of those moments.

Rachel touched the scruff along his jawline. He held her hand to his face for a second and then brought her fingers to his mouth and kissed them.

"Are you going to let him quit?" she asked.

"I don't know. That's just it. Should he stay and work through it or what? Do you think it will ever change?"

Rachel didn't know what to say. TJ was tough and usually approached life with a determination that left little room for doubt, but tonight in his eyes Rachel saw his vulnerability.

"Like I said before, he has come so far," she said. "It is easy to forget how bad things were. This season, though, it is like seeing that angry little boy again. I know he isn't fighting us or having long, angry tantrums like he used to, but I would be lying if I didn't tell you I am worried."

"Well, yeah. Me, too. Seriously. This has been the worst football season yet. And I can see it's affecting him off the field, too."

"I know," Rachel agreed. "His behavior at home is more rudimentary. Even though he isn't angry here, he seems pretty shut-down like he is simply trying to function or survive. There are days I can't see the progress for all the

Chapter 14: Heart to Heart

dysfunction he is exhibiting. I mean, he's sorta holding it together here, but he's struggling. Sometimes I am afraid it will get as bad as it was before." As she put words to her worry she felt close to tears.

TJ nodded. He chewed on his lower lip, thinking, twisting the ring on his finger. He inhaled deeply and let out a long breath. "I hoped football would be a release for him, you know? Like it was for me. But Rick's right, isn't he? We just keep acting like it's going to be okay, but he isn't getting any better out there. Every week he has more and more aggression. If we are really honest we all know it isn't working out."

"He has also had way more pressure lately." Rachel was trying to understand why this year was so different. "So many changes at once—new school, new rules, and a whole new set of kids."

TJ put his hand on her shoulder. "I really like watching him play. I like him being part of the team with me. But I don't think I should keep trying to make it work if it is making him worse."

Rachel searched his face. That was not an easy admission for TJ. Coaching his son in football was a dream he longed for, but it had turned into a nightmare. Plus TJ felt a lot of pride in how good Ben was. Again, she chose her words carefully.

"It's tough for all parents to find the balance of how much to push their kids to get better, to work through their challenges, and knowing when to let go and move in a different direction. For you to have to realize this isn't working and maybe have to let it go, that's tough. I know that is not what you wanted to happen."

"No." TJ shook his head. "It isn't going at all like I'd hoped. I figured he wanted to play bad enough that he would control his temper and learn to do what he had to do so he could play. That's what I was banking on. Coach Fischer and I both thought it was going to help him to play hard, and maybe use his anger in a positive way so he'd be more in control and become emotionally stronger. But Rache, I am there on the field with the boy, and every day it is worse."

"Yeah."

"What happens to Ben when he is out on the field is different than a kid who needs to learn to channel his aggression." TJ paused. He rubbed his chin. "I've been thinking this kind of sport, the intensity of it, the constant physical contact, somehow triggers him to a level maybe he can't control. He knows his job out there, but anyone—our team or the other team—gets in his space and he fights. I don't know what to do anymore to help him. His coach doesn't either."

"To be honest, Babe, I doubt Ben knows either. Maybe

Chapter 14: Heart to Heart

the pressure this year is just too much. To me, it seems to send him into the primal part of his brain and he can't see any options but to fight." Rachel recalled something about kids with traumatic histories. "Hey, remember the workshop we went to about helping really aggressive children?"

"Which one?"

She punched him playfully. She was sure he knew what she was talking about. He liked to pretend she dragged him to psychological workshops against his will. But there was a time when the boys were about nine and ten when she and TJ both had been desperate to find answers and they'd looked everywhere. She joked back, "It was that one you begged me to sign you up for, silly."

He grinned sheepishly. At the same time together as if on cue they quoted a truism they'd learned back then.

"If he could act better, he would."

"We need to remember that saying," Rachel said.

TJ nodded.

When the boys had first come home, TJ had been really good at just being with them and creating trust and safety. As parents, they worked together on creating an environment and family that was safe and caring for all their children. Rachel and TJ talked often about how to help the boys through their past trauma histories. Sooner than they had expected, the boys settled in and for a while things got better. They were less agitated. They were bonding and thriving.

Then it got tough again, really tough. Ben and Ricky had different struggles, but suddenly it seemed they were back to square one with temper tantrums, fighting at home, defiance, and surly back-talk.

Rachel had expected some bumps in the road, but she had to admit, it had taken her off guard. She and TJ started really feeling the strain of the chaos it was creating. There were daily battles similar to when they had first come home, but by then the boys were bigger as well as stronger, and the struggles were even more exhausting.

For Ben it was a constant fight to control every situation. His anger often tried TJ's patience and Rachel was caught in the middle between two angry males. Ricky's emotional outbursts, irrational fears and constant neediness wore them out. It didn't matter that Rachel knew so much about helping kids and families who were in similar situations; it was taking its toll on her and their marriage.

TJ was becoming more and more irritated and edgy most of the time. He felt the boys should be able to follow directions and make good choices. He was putting more pressure on her to come up with consequences or punishments. It was easy for each of them to blame the other for the problems with the boys. The turmoil was pulling them apart. Rachel knew things had to change. She couldn't hold on to what she believed about parenting and fight TJ, too.

Just when she thought she was at her breaking point she had heard about a specialist on the East Coast who worked with extremely violent children, a colleague of Dr. Bruce Perry whom Rachel relied on in her work. Even though Ben and Ricky's behaviors were not as severe as some they had heard about, she and TJ were proactive to get help before the situation became unsafe.

The conference was in line with much of what Rachel taught other families. The doctor and his team gave her and TJ the support they needed to set up a family intervention program in their home. It had kept things from getting to the point of needing inpatient care, and the program was instrumental in the boys' healing.

Thinking back on it now, Rachel knew it had been a turning point for them. They became more unified. It got them all on the same page. The changes in the family helped the boys to adjust. Their ability to trust increased and that enabled them to be calmer even under stress. Rachel shuddered to think what things would have been like if they had not made the effort to work intensely to bring change. Until this fall, the boys had been steadily getting better.

Rachel brought herself back to the present. "Well, do you think there is something in what they said about not putting the kids in high pressure, high stress situations over and over?"

"I guess so," TJ said, "although, life is full of things we have to overcome. I wish we could just help him be able to handle it. Is there a way to push through it?"

"But is football really like real life?" Rachel asked thoughtfully. "I mean in real life, there are pressures, but not so many people right in your face, physically pushing you and downright intending to hurt you. Football is pretty intense and violent, day after day."

Rachel leaned against the counter next to TJ. He was pensive, quietly considering her words. She reached for his hand. "TJ, I know you wanted your son to play ball like you did. It must be really hard to think about him quitting."

"Yeah, well, it isn't easy. I thought I could guide him through this. But I am seeing him fall apart, Babe." TJ bit on his bottom lip and then let out a deep breath. "He's more volatile than he was before. And our relationship, the one I feel I've worked so hard to build with him, it's really bad." TJ shook his head, twisting his ring.

Rachel bumped his shoulder lightly. "Want to pray with me about it? I am sure God knows what you both need."

Chapter 14: Heart to Heart

"Okay, sure. Let's do that." He took her hand. Together, they went back to the dinner table. Sitting down, TJ said, "When we are done here I think I'll just hang out with him a little. He must be feeling pretty bad after today's episode. Probably thinks I am mad at him."

Rachel smiled lovingly at him before she bowed her head.

When they had finished praying Rachel looked up to see Ben standing in the doorway watching them. She squeezed TJ's hand and gave a little nod toward Ben so TJ would notice him. Ben had a strange look on his face, a mixture of defiance and hurt, and most of all, perplexity.

"Why are you praying for me to quit football?" He sounded angry, as if they had betrayed him.

"Son—" TJ started. He got up from the table. Ben took a step back, his fists closed tightly. Rachel wondered if the boy might punch something, or perhaps even his father. "Ben." TJ's voice had a commanding tone this time, but he stopped moving. Then more gently, he said, "Ben, why don't you come in so we all can sit down and talk about it."

"No! It's not your decision. It's mine! If I want to quit I don't need you to tell me!"

Rachel could see the misunderstanding behind Ben's immediate anger. She felt the fleeting hopelessness of a situation Ben was sure would be against him. When he felt the most powerless he tended to fight the hardest.

"You want me to quit, don't you?" It was more a statement than a question. His voice was getting louder as it gained intensity. "You talked to coach and you both decided to kick me off the team even if I don't quit!" His eyes darted wildly. "You are my dad! You are supposed to stand by me!"

Rachel could see Ben's feelings were escalating to the point where he couldn't hear anything they were saying. He yelled a few explicit swear words. Her own mind raced in search of anything she could say or do to slow him down.

TJ cautiously took a step toward him. Rachel knew he was getting ready to take hold of Ben if they needed to contain him for safety reasons. TJ wasn't going to grab him unless he needed to. Both he and Rachel had experienced calming children when their emotions became overwhelming. TJ was good at being firm and clear without exacerbating the situation.

Ben stopped shouting.

Rachel could see TJ longing to connect with Ben in that moment without sending him over the edge into a full destructive rage. Ben backed up another step. He wasn't yelling, but his body was more taunt and he looked ready to fight. Rachel and TJ had learned to move in as close as

Chapter 14: Heart to Heart

they could but sometimes there was no way to close the gap. When Ben was in the fight-or-flight part of his brain, he fought any available help.

TJ just stood still. He didn't stare Ben down, and he gave all the signals he could that he wasn't going to fight. Still, Ben was tense, his eyes locked on TJ.

"You look really mad," Rachel said. She had slipped around to the side of the room so she could help if Ben bolted. At the sound of her voice, Ben looked away from TJ. He seemed surprised to see Rachel still in the room. He turned toward her. She repeated her statement, noting the darkness in his eyes now locked on hers. He didn't reply.

"You are probably too mad to talk about this." She held his eyes hoping he would see love in hers. She tried to look relaxed and sound candid. "I mean, you know we have to talk about it, but not right now. I guess. Maybe you just need more time to be really mad."

She paused. For some reason he was listening. She could see his hands relax a bit, even though his body was still tense. She kept going.

"I just wonder sometimes what you are really most angry at. What is it? This family? Your dad? Coach Fischer? The team? Me? Ricky? The whole world itself?" She measured each word, matching a bit of his anger with each possibility.

Ben dropped his head. He took a deep breath and blew it out with an irate huff. But she could tell he had shifted. Rachel wasn't sure why, but he was calmer. Meanwhile, she was inching closer to him and he wasn't backing away.

TJ carefully pulled a chair away from the table and sat down. He didn't say anything. He just sat patiently watching the two of them. It was a brilliant move because by taking the seat he took a lower stance. And it was working. Rachel could see Ben backing down. She thought of a song she had heard about how a hurt heart was guarded, and a guarded heart was always ready for a fight. Ben was clearly that.

They were quiet, the three of them. Ben looked at the floor while Rachel studied him. She occasionally glanced over at TJ. They locked eyes for a moment. She nodded slightly. They both knew a teenage-sized meltdown had been avoided. By the grace of God, Rachel thought.

Finally, TJ broke the silence. "I don't blame you, Son. I'd be furious too." TJ was composed and direct. "It probably seems like we are all against you. Why should you believe me when I tell you I want what is best for you?" TJ shook his head and chuckled. "I know if I thought someone was making me do something I sure as hell wouldn't believe it."

Ben looked at his dad. TJ dropped his head and pretended to be very busy examining his fingernail. When he glanced

Chapter 14: Heart to Heart

up, he caught Ben studying him. TJ spoke with measured ease. "You come in here and find your Mama and me praying about you and the trouble you are having on the field and off the field and asking God to help us so we can help you. I can understand that would make you mad. I know you don't like us talking about you to anybody, especially God."

TJ had Ben's attention. "You probably thought we were going over your head asking Him what we should do. Seemed like we were asking God when we hadn't even talked to you about it." TJ paused a few seconds. "I can see how that probably made you feel like we had already decided something for you without even asking you."

Rachel could see Ben was more engaged in what TJ was saying.

"It's just you didn't even talk to me about quitting," Ben said. His eyes flashed with intensity. "I know I keep screwing it all up. I can't do anything right. But all season you keep telling me how great I am, that I am doing better. 'It's all gonna be fine. Just keep working hard, Son.'"

Rachel was amazed to see Ben brush at tears with the back of his hand.

"I thought you wanted me to play no matter what."

TJ nodded. "Sounds like you wanted to quit, but you felt

like it would be letting me down."

Rachel could see TJ had hit it exactly right. Again, tears sprung in Ben's eyes, and this time he just let them fall. Rachel was sure TJ was as surprised as she was that Ben was letting his hurt show.

"I am trying really hard, Dad. I know you don't think so, but I really am." Ben threw his hands up in the air. He exhaled loudly. Looking right at TJ, he said, "I don't think I can do this." When TJ didn't react, Ben continued. "I love football, at least I did. But I hate playing on this team. It's not fun." He looked over at Rachel. "I do feel mad, all the time, at everybody."

Rachel moved quietly and sat down. She was amazed Ben was able to express himself. It wasn't that long ago he would have been yelling, swearing and breaking things.

"Ever since I made varsity I've felt out of place. You're coaching—" He extended a hand toward TJ. "—and I'm supposed to be really good. But it sucks. I don't feel good at anything. And the whole team hates me."

Ben said all this quickly, his words coming out in broken sentences and tumbling over each other, tears still falling fitfully. He poured out his struggles with football, school and being part of a team. He paced and gestured. He was loud and occasionally swore.

Chapter 14: Heart to Heart

Rachel and TJ listened, nodding now and then in empathy. They didn't judge his words, or the way he was expressing himself. Rachel was sure TJ felt as relieved as she at this new outpouring of Ben's thoughts, feelings and fears.

Finally, Ben stopped talking and pacing. He stood still. He looked worn out.

"I had no idea you felt this way," TJ said. "I feel bad I put that kind of pressure on you."

Ben looked at him then at Rachel. She told him she agreed with TJ that she hadn't realized how hard it had been for him.

"Well, now I hear you all talking like maybe I should quit," Ben said, now more calm. "But that—that makes me mad, too. I don't know why. It's just—I don't know. Nothing I do is going to be right."

"Maybe you feel we should have helped you more with this, um, struggle, or battle you have been in," Rachel commented. "You know, instead of us not talking about it. Did you think we left you to try and deal with this on your own?"

Rachel threw it out there even though Ben was the one who had chosen not to talk about the struggles he was having. She had found with kids it didn't hurt to take a guess at what they might be thinking. If she was wrong Ben would correct her.

"I think you thought we were dead set on making sure you didn't quit," TJ said. "What we meant to be support was actually more pressure. Is that how you felt?"

Ben shrugged. He didn't offer any answers, but he was listening. TJ was being careful in what he said. Rachel and he had learned through the years to take it slow and easy after a child started to calm down. Once they got through a meltdown it wasn't too hard to send them back into a fit of rage. Countless times Rachel had seen parents, teachers or childcare workers try to deal with a child too soon after a meltdown. That was a huge mistake because the child could not yet process their behavior. Sometimes you had to let the dust settle and approach the child in more subtle ways. It was best to listen and work on connecting.

"Truth is," TJ said slowly. "I really hadn't thought about you quitting the team. I didn't know you were even thinking about it until I heard you say it to Coach Fischer today."

"Well," Ben began hesitantly, "most of the time I don't want to quit." He moved closer to the table. "I just don't feel like I'm doing any good at anything. School is hard, too—" Ben chuckled a little the way TJ often did. "—but you probably won't let me quit that."

Rachel laughed, too. "Probably right on that one. But we would like to help you."

Chapter 14: Heart to Heart

"What if I really can't do it though?" Ben looked down and was quiet. He shifted his weight uneasily. Rachel could tell something else was going through his mind. When no one said anything, he looked up and said somewhat nervously, "Umm, you are going to be really mad when you see how bad my grades are. I haven't been keeping up with school. I am not sure Coach would even let me play when he finds out."

"But you have to turn in a grade check each Friday before the game—signed by all your teachers," TJ said. "I've seen yours. It's been okay."

Ben sucked in a big breath of air and squared his shoulders as he exhaled. "I changed the grades after the teachers signed it." He hurriedly added, "I only did it last week, but—"

Rachel saw TJ also take a deep breath. He hated cheating. And he hated lying more than anything. Unfortunately, for most kids with trust issues lying was a common behavior. Almost every adoptive family Rachel had worked with dealt with lying on some level. Ben had been a huge storyteller when he was younger. TJ had worked really hard to build trust with him so he could be honest. Even after years learning to deal with this in Ben it was still a challenge for TJ to handle. All their kids had learned TJ was usually way more upset by the lie than the behavior that motivated it. The bad grades would have been less an issue for TJ than the deceitful way Ben tried to hide them.

TJ turned to Rachel with a now-what-do-I-do look. She could see he didn't trust himself to address this right now. They had been taught through parenting hurt kids, to create safety and not overreact to a lie. It was time to put what she knew into practice so Ben would continue to be honest in this moment.

Rachel moved from the table and stood close to Ben, eye to eye but still as non-threatening as possible.

"Ben, I can see this has probably been bothering you for a while."

Ben didn't speak, but he didn't pull away either.

"It hurts me and Daddy because we really want you to trust us. It scares me when you lie and cheat because it reminds me you don't trust us yet."

Her words hung in the air. No one said anything. Rachel thought about how difficult the last few weeks had been. If she had been looking for it, she probably would have realized he was covering up and lying. His deceitfulness was like a splinter, festering into outward behavior when he was hiding things. She wondered, was he sabotaging his grades so he wouldn't have to play? Or was he out of sorts from his problems on the football field and therefore unable to keep it together in school? Either way, he had been trying to deal with it secretly.

Chapter 14: Heart to Heart

In line with Rachel's approach, TJ stood and rested his hand on Ben's shoulder. "Son, why don't we sleep on it? Think you can do that? We can talk about it more tomorrow night."

"So, am I supposed to go to practice like nothing is going on?" Ben asked.

"Hmm. It seems you've already been doing that." TJ spoke firmly yet gently. "Son, I know you need to be in control of what is happening. My guess is you didn't just let your grades slip. Maybe you were using the poor grades to get off the team, or maybe you hoped that by cheating on the grade check you might have to leave school. I don't know for sure, but I do know it goes against your nature to cover up and hide stuff. You weren't built for lying and sneaking around. Living like that eats you up from the inside out. You hate feeling powerless and out of control. But when you live in the shadows of lies and half-truths you lose control of making decisions and working things through because life becomes about hoping you don't get found out."

Ben hung his head. TJ waited until he looked up. "Son, it hurts me, too, that you don't trust us enough to help you with tough stuff like this. I don't think there is anything more we can say or do tonight." He turned to Rachel. "Do you?"

Rachel agreed they needed some time. She looked at

Ben and waited for him to look at her. It was quiet for a long while. Finally, Ben shrugged. "Yeah, whatever." She watched as he walked away. No matter how flippant his "whatever" seemed, she could see clearly he was carrying the weight of all that had been said on his shoulders.

CHAPTER 15
From Ben's Journal

It's not that I don't want to do the right thing. I do. And it's not that I want to make everyone around me pissed off. I don't. But for all the good in me there is nothing stronger than whatever it is that gets me in trouble over and over. Even if I do good for a while it comes to a crashing halt. I mess up in so many ways. Then I completely lose it and cuss out a teacher or hit someone on my team or do something just as dumb.

When it's happening I am not thinking about doing something wrong or right, and I sure don't think about what is going to happen next. I just let whatever is inside me take over. Then later I hate myself for it. Lately, I have been hating myself a lot.

I don't know if I can play football, finish school or ever really make it. Right now I am hating everything about me. I feel like crap most of the time, and sometimes the only relief is in the middle of doing what I later feel even more crappy *about. When I am mad and yelling at Kyle or throwing stuff around in my room, in that moment I feel better. How weird is that? Maybe I am just too screwed up to be good.*

My dad has been telling me not to quit the football team. Daddy says I need to work through it and tough it out. I know my coach wants to kick me off. He sure said as much today. But even though he threatens to throw me off the team he also tells me he wants me to hang in there. They both think I can do this. But deep inside me, I don't know if I can.

So maybe that's why I have been trying to get in trouble with school and grades or something so I can get off the team without it being about football. I hadn't really thought about it like that before, but when I wrote it down, it kind of fits. Damn.

CHAPTER 16
Fear Is Easy: Love Is Hard

There were no easy answers for Ben with football and his academic struggles. He had told TJ and Rachel his low grades were recent, but Rachel found out the next week they'd been below par for more than a month. In fact, he had been caught cheating on a test and copying another student's homework.

He was plenty smart enough to handle the workload. Sadly, trying to be helpful, the teachers had been giving him a lot of leeway, not holding him accountable or informing Rachel about his difficulties. When Rachel asked why she had not been notified about his failing grades his counselor said the school was just giving Ben time to adjust. They did not want to trouble TJ or Rachel about problems they were handling at school. The counselor seemed to be focused on placating Rachel, patting her hand condescendingly and telling her she didn't need to be bothered about it.

Rachel could see that more than a few allowances had been made. The school had not been upholding their own policies in regard to academic standards and extracurricular activities. She suspected it was because Ben was Troy Keyton's son.

For any school, especially a private Christian school, it had to be tempting to simply smooth things over rather than risk offending one of their primary donors. They also might have been more lenient because the Keytons had been a part of the Heritage school family for years. Whatever the reason, she and TJ had not been told about Ben's problems.

That evening TJ and Rachel walked hand in hand toward the old barn where they frequently met when they wanted privacy. Rachel pulled her sweater tightly around her body to keep warm. Typically October was still pleasant, but it was nearly November and once the sun went down there was the breath of winter in the air.

Rachel had met TJ in the garage when he pulled in after practice. He sent the boys in to clean up for dinner so the two of them could talk about what she had found out from the school. TJ had wanted to see how Ben did at practice this week so no decisions as to whether he would quit or not had been made.

Rachel had spent the better part of the afternoon at the school. When she told TJ the extent of the problems he was livid.

"I can't believe their high standards and school policies would allow them to keep us in the dark. To just blow off Ben's grades and behaviors seems so damn deception." TJ threw his arms up in the air. "That's just not right!"

Chapter 16: *Fear is Easy: Love is Hard*

"I know," Rachel said quietly. "I thought we made it clear we needed to stay on top of things with Ben and Ricky. Maybe they thought we knew how he was doing. Maybe they thought we were covering for him, too."

"Yeah, well. Damn it. Now what? He is really behind! Do you think he can dig himself out of this hole?" TJ ran his hand through his hair and then placed his cap back on. "We need to talk about this with Ben."

"Yeah. I just wanted you to have some time to process things beforehand. I thought you might need to blow off a little steam before you talked to him—or to the school. I know I need to. It's not going to help Ben if we are angry with the school. I'm upset with them and I sure don't want to talk about it with him yet."

They walked silently for a few moments. Rachel thought about how to convey her disappointment and anger with the way the school had handled things. TJ was a loyal Heritage supporter and she didn't want him to feel defensive. But she was irritated and upset with how they had handled Ben. From the start she had felt the private school—where the students were from mostly upper-middleclass families—might not be a good fit for the boys. Although there were many things she liked about the school, she was a lot more willing than TJ to go elsewhere.

"You know, TJ," she started carefully, "when Ben was at the public school I always felt I was part of the team. There was respect, you know, for me as a therapist and for the work I do. They also seemed to respect us as parents and what we wanted. But today at Heritage I felt outside their system. And I realized I have always felt that way even when the girls went there. The teachers were standoffish and the administration seemed to have their own agenda. The girls did fine, but I remember when my three first started I wasn't too sure about it. When I had you or Tina there people were generally friendly. It took a long time though before I felt anyone knew me when you weren't around." Rachel paused. She hoped TJ could understand what she was feeling.

"I need them to see me as a parent, not the famous Troy Keyton's wife. I didn't think about it much until today, but after all these years, I still feel a bit like an outsider when I am there without you."

TJ stopped and faced her. "Why didn't you tell me this before?"

"I guess I figured it was just me, you know? You and Tina had been there so long. With the girls, really, I was seldom there without you. Besides, I am sort of used to being in your shadow. The girls were happy there and that's what mattered to me. They were benefiting from the school and the situation. My own discomfort wasn't getting in the way.

Chapter 16: Fear is Easy; Love is Hard

It wasn't something I thought about much."

"In my shadow?" TJ shook his head. "Really, is that how you feel? Because when it comes to the kids—yours or mine, or any kids—I feel like I am just trying to follow your lead."

They started walking again. Rachel silently took TJ's hand. She heard him inhale deeply, and she took a deep breath, too. They exhaled together. She loved being near him. As strong as she was as a woman, she still found solace in his strength. His depth of character gave her someone to lean on and take refuge in.

At the old barn, TJ leaned against his old pick-up truck and pulled Rachel close to him.

With him so near, it was tempting to put troubling thoughts on the back burner. But she knew there were issues they had to address. She thought about how different things had been with the girls' schooling than it was raising the boys.

"TJ, the truth is, I've never had to deal with the school—any school—as much as I have had to with the boys. I'm not used to my kids being in so much trouble. When we started the boys at the public school we knew it was going to require all of us working together toward our goals. I really didn't have many interactions with Heritage much then. I think you were on that end so I hadn't really faced how it was all playing out there. Now I definitely feel like I am on their turf—and yours—at this school."

Rachel thought about Ben's years in public school and all the times she had been called in to help with him, or even other children.

"At other schools I felt I was treated as an equal. Even with the boys' schooling, I was part of Ben's and Ricky's team. And I have to say, I was treated better."

TJ blew a breath through his nose. "Damn. Where have I been?"

"Uh, coaching and being super-dad. Duh." Rachel nudged him good-naturedly.

"How's that been working?" TJ returned her love tap then got a serious look. "Honestly, Rache, it isn't working, is it? I mean, I thought we could get the boys stable and they could go to school there like the girls had. I like coaching and being part of things at Heritage, but I seriously had no idea we were getting 'special' treatment. I sure as hell don't like that you feel out of the loop or don't feel respected."

"It's not a big problem on my part, Babe. It's not like it upsets me on a regular basis. Well, until now. Today I was upset. I just don't know if the school is really going to work for us. Maybe if I get more assertive they might handle things differently. But to be perfectly honest, I don't know if I can

Chapter 16: Fear is Easy: Love is Hard

handle them not respecting my position. I mean, when I say I need something to happen it comes from my experience and my expertise as well as being a parent. If the administration can't regard what I bring to the table it's going to be a battle."

Rachel paused, trying to clarify her thoughts. "I'm not sure fighting to get them to see what is really going on with kids from troubled situations is where I want to spend my energy. I want the school to respect my experience enough to recognize that what I think isn't just a whim. There are some things I know work that others don't know, especially with Ben."

She scanned TJ's face to see his reaction. "I mean, if this school is the best choice for Ben and Ricky I will work hard to make sure my voice is heard. Figuring out the best situation for them is so much more important than my bruised ego."

"Yeah. And what is that best situation?" TJ muttered.

"Well, to quote my favorite cowboy," Rachel grinned, "'Damned if I know!' But we better figure it out soon before that kid does something worse to ensure they throw him out."

"You think he will?"

"Oh yeah," Rachel said ruefully. "I had a client whose parents thought he really wanted to go to this private school in Colorado. They had homeschooled him until ninth grade.

They talked about it with him for a couple years, you know, to prepare him. He even had to write an essay about why he wanted to go. The family even had to get a grant and it was a long process. He did everything as though he wanted to attend that school. But once he got there he felt really out of place. There weren't any kids he knew. He was struggling to keep up and fit in. He didn't feel he could tell his parents how out of place he felt and how much he hated it. So he started changing his image, trying to feel comfortable. Ultimately, he was hanging out with a kid that brought pot to school. They smoked it in the other kid's car at lunch and both ended up getting kicked out. The boy was sent to the local high school. By the time he was able to talk about the whole experience he said the public school was where he had wanted to go all along." Rachel put her hand up. "I know, I know. Why didn't he just tell them? But sometimes we can't verbalize all that is going on or even come up with a rationale we think might be plausible."

"So you think Ben wants to go back to public school?"

"I don't know."

"And what about Rick? Do we send him back too or keep him at Heritage?"

"I don't know about that either. Has Rick really found his place at Heritage? And once you give the school a piece of your mind, like I know you want to, will this be a school we feel confident continuing with?"

"You're supposed to answer my questions, girl, not ask more!"

"I'm just saying—"

TJ nodded. "Yeah, I hear ya. I guess we need to talk to Heritage and to Ben and maybe to Rick, too. I'll do whatever, alright? Maybe it was naïve to think Ben would magically fit in with this school and these kids. And maybe Rick is stressed out, too."

"Or maybe just taking football out of it will help Ben enough." Rachel suggested. "He might just need a year to grow up a bit more, feel more comfortable. We don't know for sure what it would be like if he wasn't on the team with all that pressure."

"But that still doesn't account for you feeling like we don't have a good team here in helping him," TJ pointed out. "I don't take the way you feel about that lightly, Rache."

"Maybe we need to start with the school then. I mean, I have been pretty laid back with them until now. I can be more assertive. If I come in and request a meeting, kind of take charge of this, we can see how they handle it. If they are willing to have us involved on a different level we can all pull together on making it work for Ben, and for Rick, too."

They started back toward the house. It was dark, cold and quiet. Rachel looked up at the evening sky. She silently prayed they would have the wisdom and the grace to know what to do. TJ took her hand in his firm, warm grasp. "You're cold," he said and tucked her arm under his. He covered her hand with his other one and gently rubbed it.

"The main thing, remember, is to create safety," he said.

She remembered. It was their motto when they didn't know what to do with the boys or how to help them through really difficult situations. They had heard over and over how deep-rooted fear and lack of trust is built into kids from traumatic pasts. Their behaviors often covered over their need to feel safe. Rachel and TJ had taken this to heart in their home. When they struggled with how to help one of their kids or where a boundary should be they went back to this and asked, "How can we build trust and connection here?"

Rachel leaned against him as they walked along the stone path to the doorway. She was reminded of how bumpy the journey of family, of life, could be. As soon as you think one thing is going better something else comes up. "Never a dull moment," her mother used to say. She smiled up at TJ as he held the door open for her. No matter what big or small

Chapter 16: Fear is Easy: Love is Hard

decisions lay before them Rachel was certain between the two of them they would figure it out.

CHAPTER 17
Good Fight

It didn't take long for TJ to set up a meeting with the school. In fact, within the week Rachel, TJ, Coach Fischer, Principal Marc Harper, Ms. Brookes, the school counselor, and some of Ben's teachers sat around a conference table to discuss what would be best for Ben, and ultimately, the Keyton family.

Not being a public school, Heritage did not offer Individual Educational Plan (IEP) services needed by emotionally disturbed children. Ben had actually been handling school without an IEP for several years. Neither he nor Rick had diagnoses that qualified them for such services.

Rachel felt hopeful. First of all, the school had been very agreeable to meeting. It may have had to do with TJ's presence, but he and Rachel had decided if it took his clout to make the school hear them out TJ would use it. So he had approached the principal about scheduling the meeting.

He let Mr. Harper know he and Rachel were upset and were thinking of pulling the boys out of the school. It wasn't a threat; it was a real possibility. He said they needed more support than the school seemed able to give, but left it open for Harper to come up with ideas to make things work. Rachel received a call from Ms. Brookes setting up a meeting two days later between herself, the coach, and of course, the administration.

Meanwhile, at home, Rachel and TJ talked to the boys. They had learned from past experience that being open about what was going on, especially if it involved change, was the best format. First, they talked to Rick and asked how he was feeling about the school. He never brought friends home or seemed to be close to anyone his age.

Ricky expressed that he really liked his teachers, loved playing tennis on the team, and that he got along well with everyone on his cross country team. He didn't want to switch schools, but he would if Ben wanted to. That is how it was with Rick. Rachel knew they had to watch out with him because his problems were more internalized. He was more likely to give up what he wanted and then be depressed or moody. Rachel told TJ later that even if they did end up moving Ben to a different school, it might be best to keep Ricky at Heritage.

That evening after dinner Ben hung around while Rachel washed dishes and tidied up the kitchen. Ben was funny that way. He was almost clingy at times. He was so strong fighting for control and independence that it was easy to think he didn't care about anyone else.

Chapter 17: Good Fight

When he was younger he would go out of his way to exert this power and control. While he was particularly slow to accept Rachel as his mother, there were times—like this evening—when he would cuddle up to her, letting his neediness show. She and TJ had worked hard to make sure he had to connect with Rachel to get needs met. As he began to feel safe at home and more attached he was more affectionate, at least before he hit fourteen.

Now he mostly displayed his tough guy side. But he still occasionally sidled up to Rachel in the kitchen. Most of the children Rachel worked with had similar attachment issues causing them to alternately push away and pull their parents in close. Ben had grown by leaps and bounds, but he still struggled with relationships, even at home.

Since he was standing nearby, Rachel asked Ben to help her put the clean dishes away. She could tell he wanted to be close, but wasn't sure if he felt like talking. She found working side by side often helped ease his awkwardness and loosen his tongue.

"Hey Mama," he said, putting the ketchup into the fridge, "will Daddy still coach the football team if I stop playing?"

Rachel stole a glance at him and saw he'd stopped to look at her. She pretended to be busy wiping the counter.

"I mean, it will be kind of weird either way, right? If I stop playing and he keeps coaching? Or if we both quit? The guys are going to be so mad at me."

Rachel kept moving slowly, thoughtfully. "Hmm. I think your daddy is really mostly concerned about how things are for you. I don't think he's thought yet what he will do. Sounds like you have been thinking about this a lot though. I guess he could finish out the season either way. But it kind of depends on if you stay at Heritage even more than if you play ball or not."

"What?" He stopped what he was doing. "What do you mean? I might not go to school? I thought this was all about football." He swallowed hard. "But what about Ricky? Will we both have to leave?"

"Ben, we haven't decided anything. Remember the other day we said we needed to talk about all the options? You aren't getting kicked out or sent away. We are just talking about if Heritage is the right school for you. Maybe it was too much of a change. But we haven't decided anything for sure. We are just throwing options out there."

She glanced at Ben to see how he was reacting. He had started putting things in the dishwasher.

"So," she asked casually, "am I hearing you say you don't want to change schools?"

Chapter 17: *Good Fight*

"No!" Ben was adamant. "I didn't even know that was going to be a possibility. I just thought it was about playing football or not."

Rachel fell silent. She had a lot to say, but she didn't want to overwhelm him with a lot of conversation. Even though she wanted to ask him a ton of questions about his thoughts and feelings she knew she needed to let him think things through. They were both silent for a while. Ben chewed on his lower lip. Rachel stole glances at him while she straightened things up in the dishwasher. He looked so much like TJ when he was thinking hard about something.

"Well, can I go to Heritage without playing football, can't I?" he finally asked.

"Certainly. No one is making you play. We want you to feel comfortable, Ben."

"Oh. I thought maybe you all were thinking if I went to a different school it would be easier for me to play football and keep up with my school work. Like last year." He seemed to be studying his hands, picking at his fingernails. Rachel was certain there was more he wanted to say. She waited.

"I don't want to tell Daddy I don't want to play on his team." He looked up at Rachel, his eyes starting to fill with tears. He was so rarely emotional that Rachel wanted to be careful not to say or do anything to cause more hurt or confusion. She didn't say anything right away. Instead, she slowly folded the dish towel. She hoped he would not shut down.

Finally, she said, "Your dad and I want you to feel safe and secure. If you enjoy playing ball and it helps you to feel part of the team then we want you to play." She tried to catch his eye, but he kept his head down.

"Ben, you are a hard worker. You don't quit anything easily, even when you need to. You're stubborn that way, just like your daddy. But I know your dad isn't set on you playing if it isn't working for you. Honestly, Ben, something isn't working right now. I don't know if it's about football or about this particular school. Or maybe it's just something going on inside you."

She put her hand on his shoulder. "Sometimes quitting is harder than staying. It means letting go and saying there is something else you need more. I am not sure if this makes sense to you. Quitting is hard. I understand that and so does your father."

They stood close together for a long moment without talking at all. Ben didn't move away from her as he sometimes did. He let her stay close with her hand on his shoulder while he thought about what she had said.

Then he nodded and stepped away. "Okay. But I don't

Chapter 17: Good Fight

want to change schools. Except for the football team I sort of like this school." Rachel nodded but let him continue. He got an impish grin and looked her straight in the eye. "The girls are much hotter at Heritage, so I want to stay, okay?"

Rachel laughed. "I'm not sure you want that to be your persuasive argument!" She reached up and ruffled his hair. "Wise-guy. Okay, fine. I'll keep that in mind."

He started out of the kitchen then turned back toward her. "Mama, are you going to tell Daddy about what I said? About not changing schools, I mean?"

"Well, he needs to know your thoughts on this, and soon. You can go talk to him, too, or I can give him the run down on what you think. We are meeting with the school this week to talk about everything."

"You can tell him. Just don't tell him about the girls, okay? I don't want another lecture about the birds and the bees."

Rachel laughed heartily. "Oh, Ben." She shook her head. "You should probably tell him yourself about not wanting to play football. I think that would be the most mature thing to do. Are you sure you won't let me tell him your true reason for wanting to stay?"

He shook his head obstinately.

She smiled at his boyishness. "Awe, so unfair."

"Fine." He tried to look serious. But as he turned away and headed down the stairs to where TJ was he couldn't contain a smile. "Whatever," he called to her.

Going into this meeting knowing they would do whatever it took to keep the boys at Heritage changed the direction of the gathering for Rachel. Since she knew the boys wanted to stay she knew she would need to advocate for them to make it work. Having TJ with her, understanding her, gave Rachel confidence that they were united in what they needed from the school.

Rachel and TJ were able to explain to the school staff what they felt would help the boys to be successful. They seemed willing to listen. TJ made sure they understood the value he (and other schools the boys had attended) placed in Rachel as a therapist working with challenging children as well as the boys' mother. They agreed stronger communication was necessary between all of them. Then they explored ideas to help Ben to stay on track. TJ decided to finish out the month working with the football team. They discussed the realities of Ben quitting the team and if that would in the long run make things more or less difficult for him.

"He loves the game, and I think he might want to play again at some point," TJ told Coach Fischer. "Well, maybe," he equivocated. "This isn't the first team he's struggled with. In fact, he hasn't been able to hold it together on the field for

Chapter 17: Good Fight

any team. The real problem this time is that it was affecting him off the field even more than on the field. On the positive side, this time Ben was able to see it wasn't working. It will be interesting to see how not playing helps him overall."

Rachel agreed with TJ. She talked to the group about how stress impacts the brain and how difficult it is for Ben and other kids who are in or have been through trauma to regulate themselves. One of the teachers asked about another student that was struggling in similar ways. Rachel shared some ideas on creating a sense of safety in the classroom.

The school counselor leaned over to Principal Harper. "We should have Mrs. Keyton come do an in-service for us about this. I bet it would help us with all the students."

After sitting in on countless meetings between staff and parents, Rachel knew things did not always turn out favorably. During her twenty years as a therapist helping parents navigate the school systems for their challenging children, Rachel found a shocking number of schools unwilling to learn new ways to build structure, safety and handle discipline. Thankfully, in recent years the trend seemed to be changing for the better. More information about trauma and its effects on children's ability to learn was being implemented. Trauma-sensitive education was becoming a focus for many American schools across the nation. Unwillingness to change and short-sighted refusal to come to grips with the surprising numbers of children from hard places who needed to feel safe before they could learn were becoming more the exception than the rule.

Rachel was grateful to find Heritage open to a different approach. It gave her hope. She knew if the school leaned toward a positive, supportive environment, all the students would benefit. It was difficult to convince a school—especially one as successful as Heritage—that what would help handful of challenging children would ultimately create a better learning environment for all their students.

The research was overwhelming and Rachel was happy to have worked with many staff members at schools in Colorado and Tennessee to implement changes. She was pleased that Heritage was willing to have this conversation, to see her boys as individuals and to ask good questions. Rachel and TJ left the meeting both feeling good about the boys staying at Heritage.

CHAPTER 18
Must Be Doing Something Right

"Lucky thirteen," Rachel thought as she lay back on her towel on the Jamaican beach. Twelve years ago Rachel and TJ had gotten married in a condo right off this very beach after meeting just a year earlier. On one hand she felt like she had known TJ her whole life and at the same time, it hardly seemed possible it had already been thirteen years since they first met.

As the sun warmed Rachel's skin memories of the music and dancing warmed her inside. They didn't get to be here nearly as often as they'd like, but every time they returned to this beach it reminded her of the love and laughter of their wonderful family and friends.

TJ had certainly surprised her with this anniversary retreat. It was several weeks before their real anniversary. Unfortunately, the actual date usually fell during Thanksgiving week, making it difficult for them to get away. It was tough for both her and TJ to take time out of their hectic lives any time, but near big family holidays it was almost impossible. She wasn't sure how TJ had managed to surprise her every year, but one way or another he always seemed to come up with something special for the two of them.

In the early years, after the boys had come home, there was precious little time for getting away or even being alone for that matter. For many years the Ben and, especially Ricky did not travel well, nor could they handle changes to the schedule. Whenever she or TJ was away, the boys struggled. Both boys had incredibly deep attachment issues. Even if things went fine while they were gone, the fallout from the disruption hit hard when they returned. So they'd gotten used to staying pretty close to home.

Ricky and Ben, each in his own way, had layers of fear about people leaving. It had taken consistency and time to reassure them this family was forever. Consequently, TJ and Rachel found ways to connect and celebrate without venturing too far away—quiet dinners, camping out in their own bedroom, romantic overnights in local hotels or at cute bed and breakfasts. Sometimes TJ would wake her in the middle of the night and invite her to join him outside to look at the stars cuddled together in a blanket.

He was an artist truly, in the ways he found to make her feel wanted and special, a master of simple pleasures. He continually reminded her and the kids that he loved and cared for them in a thousand small, thoughtful ways. Rachel was giving and loving, one hundred percent loyal to her family, but TJ was the one who kept the adventure and spark going. If anyone asked, Rachel readily admitted without question that TJ was the romantic.

Chapter 18: Must Be Doing Something Right

Although he had done these little things for his first wife and their daughters long before Rachel knew him, it was all new for Rachel. She had been in a terrible marriage years before. And being a single parent, she was used to being taken for granted. She had to learn to be loved. TJ was the best she had ever had and she appreciated how simple and easy he made it seem.

She smiled now thinking about something he had said in an interview years ago. They asked how he managed living in a house full of girls. He told them it worked to his advantage to keep them happy and feeling special. With a knowing wink at the host, he said the best way to meet his own needs was to make his wife feel loved and wanted. The host agreed, confessing that his own wife would be happier if he actually played the romance card more often.

Rachel sat up and applied a bit more sunscreen to her arms and legs. Whatever TJ's motives, she felt the years lost to her ex-husband Mark had been made up ten-fold in the way TJ treated her. And yes, it did work, because she had never been so alive with passion for anyone as she was for TJ. Her response to his thoughtfulness was genuine and full.

She turned over so the sun could reach her back. "Rache, you are a blessed woman," she told herself. The surprise of ending up here this week made it all the more fun. She recounted the events that led her to this get-away.

A month earlier TJ had told her he had some business to attend to in California. He'd asked if she would be able to accompany him. It took some juggling clients and preparing the kids, but Rachel had been eager for the opportunity. The fast approaching holidays and the strain of their chaotic fall made getting away seem even more appealing. She swiftly cleared her schedule.

He had told her to plan for a few days, knowing full well that she scheduled all her clients early in the week so the latter part was free for family life. TJ had arranged for the boys to stay with Uncle Mike and Aunt Tina and for the older kids and Tucker to cover things at home. Telling Rachel to pack light with lots of clothes for warm, sunny weather was the only instructions he had given her. TJ had packed a few more things he knew she would need and didn't tell her until they were on their way that he was not actually taking her on a business trip.

"Really?" she asked. "No business? We can just play and sightsee in California?"

"Well, actually, we aren't going to California either." Smiling, he told her they'd be spending the week at their Jamaican condo, just the two of them.

"We haven't been there since we took the boys and all the kids, spouses and grandkids probably about five years ago!"

Chapter 18: Must Be Doing Something Right

She practically squealed with delight. Thinking about how long it had been, she said, "Yes, that's right because it was when Laney got married and they had their wedding on the beach. Wow, those were five fast years!"

TJ agreed with her about how quickly time passed.

"Lots more grandkids now," he added. "You know, we should get everyone to the condo every five years or so, don't you think?"

Rachel laughed because he was already planning the next big family adventure.

When they got to the little cottage Rachel inhaled the salty sea breeze. As soon as TJ opened the door a fresh floral fragrance wafted invitingly through the room. TJ had ordered thirteen vases of flowers, a dozen in each, her favorite daisies and roses. Rachel took in the delightful familiar smells and simple beauty of their little home away from home.

TJ stood back and watched her. She so loved this little place of theirs by the ocean and the memories that filled her were as fragrant as those that filled her senses. Turning to him, she laughed at the grin he was trying to suppress. She wrapped her arms around him and looked up to meet his eyes, twinkling with delight.

"What?" he joked. "Did I do something right?"

No answer was necessary. She kissed him passionately, both of them lost for a moment as worries melted and pressures faded away.

Finally, TJ pulled back with a groan of desire that matched hers. "Yep, I guess we know where this is going." He ran his hand through the back of his hair to gain composure. She stood close. TJ touched her face gently and pulled her against him. It didn't matter they had been married twelve years, saw each other every day, or had kids who thought they were way too old for romance.

He held her, both of them lost in the moment. They had shared their very first night as husband and wife in this exact place and the intensity of his kiss was no less than she remembered. Rachel felt her own desire mount and she simply melted into his arms.

"Come on, Babe," he whispered, his voice husky with passion. He took her hand and led her to the welcoming bedroom, their luggage and bags of groceries forgotten. He reached back and closed the door behind her.

Rachel laughed softly at his eagerness. "Guess we'll take care of our stuff later." She remembered the bags still in the rental car and piled by the front door.

"First things first," he breathed against her neck. Then he was all she thought about.

Chapter 18: *Must Be Doing Something Right*

Later, she mused how his touch, the way he loved her and made love to her felt so—complete. She was absolutely infatuated with him, something she would never have believed possible in marriage. She knew him better than she knew anyone. She knew his strengths and his weaknesses. And she felt completely known, too. They had their struggles, their miscommunications and their annoyances. At times they had different ideas about life, how to raise their kids and how to live it all out. But oh, how wonderful it could be!

Rachel thought that one of the greatest joys of her marriage was that she and TJ both really enjoyed just being together. Sure, they relished getting away and having fun, vacations and time alone, but they also both valued the day-to-day life they shared. When they walked side by side to the barn, or enjoyed a cup of coffee on a Saturday morning Rachel often felt just as complete in their compatibility and togetherness.

Rachel sat up and combed her fingers through her hair as she considered the way he had surprised her with this trip. She had to give him credit for being the one who really kept their marriage alive with surprises and fun. She was the master scheduler. TJ called her "the efficiency expert," the one who kept things running smoothly, at least as smoothly as possible. But he was the one who never took their love for granted. She loved him for it.

The waves hit the shore and the seagulls squabbled over

something down the beach. Then she lay back and let the late morning sun sooth her off to sleep.

"Hey, Babe." She opened her eyes to TJ bent over her, his hand touching hers gently so as not to startle her. "Want to wander around the island with me today?"

She shielded her eyes and smiled up at him.

"You looked so comfortable," he continued. "I came by after jogging 'bout twenty minutes ago, but decided not to wake you." Rachel reached her hand up for him to help her to her feet.

"Yeah, I think you kept me up too late last night, Mister Keyton."

They had ordered food in and watched old movies. As was their habit when they found time to be alone, they soaked in simply being together without distraction late into the night.

"No regrets here, Ma'am." He smiled into her eyes and brushed her hair from her face. "Have to spend every minute I can alone with you. You know, with each anniversary, our house gets more chaotic over the holidays. There's a good chance I might not see you again until after the first of the year."

Rachel laughed, but it was true. With kids and spouses and grandkids and friends coming by from Thanksgiving

Chapter 18: *Must Be Doing Something Right*

through New Year's, the house became a swirling mass of people. She loved it, and she treasured how their family continue to grow. However, TJ was right about how busy it was, and how scarce time alone became.

They started walking arm and arm down the beach, the sound of the waves filling in the spaces where there were no words. Rachel felt inexpressibly happy. Sometimes when life was really difficult it could feel like a series of broken promises and unmet demands. But in this moment Rachel was thinking about how fulfilled she was and how beautiful her family and her life with TJ had become.

Rachel turned to TJ with contented anticipation. "Hey, Babe—"

"Hmmm?"

"Do you remember what you promised me right before we made love the first time?"

Rachel slowed a bit as she searched his face. She thought she saw a smile behind the serious expression. He appeared contemplative, trying to mask his mischievous grin with mock gravity. But his eyes sparkled with mischief.

"I don't remember much," he answered dreamily, "except how incredible you were. Besides, you should know by now, whatever a guy promises before lovemaking is only about getting laid." He said it seriously, but he couldn't contain his goofy grin, and he darted out of reach as Rachel countered by slapping his arm playfully. She gave him her best glare.

"What?" he asked. "Oh, come on, you know it's true." He winked.

Rachel pointed his finger at him. "You know what, Mister?" She tried not to smile, but she couldn't keep a straight face. "You're such a guy."

"You got that right," he said smugly. "I just want to make you close your eyes," he crooned, quoting a song they both liked. "Was that the promise?" He darted away again from her attempt to whack him. She chased him a few steps then he stopped, turned around and caught her in his embrace.

"Okay, okay. But to quote a good friend," TJ said, "Keep in mind, 'I'm still a guy.' But, Baby, you know it would never change the promise I made you." He looked her over, his voice serious. "I swore to you I would do whatever it took to make sure you fell in love with me over and over."

Rachel smiled up at him.

"See, I do remember." He kissed her lightly. "How am I doing so far?"

Rachel didn't say anything for a moment. She pretended to grow serious. It was her turn to play a little joke on him.

Chapter 18: Must Be Doing Something Right

She gave him a deep penetrating stare. In a somber tone she said, "TJ?"

She felt him tense just a little at her change in tone.

"What?" He looked worried. Rachel didn't answer. She could tell he was uneasy. He shifted his feet uncomfortably in the sand. He was trying to figure out what he could have done to upset her and how to fix it. She tried not to grin when he began to stammer a bit. She could see he presumed he had hurt her feelings by being too flippant about their promise to love and cherish one another.

"Hey?" he tried again. "Rache, I'm sorry about that wise crack. Honest. I know it's important to you."

Rachel looked down, but he lifted her chin to meet his eyes. "Baby, I could never forget you asking me that night if I thought we would always love—no, be in love with—each other, if I thought it was possible as we grew older. I think about you asking me that—a lot, actually."

"Really?" She raised an eyebrow. "You do?"

"Yes, I do." TJ was very serious. "When you asked me, it came from this part of you that seemed so hurt. I guess I wanted to be that rescuer who could prove to you we could keep falling in love. I wanted to fix it for you." He paused and again he shifted uneasily. "Now I'm kind'a afraid to ask how I'm doing."

She reached up and touched his face gently. "I was going to tease you about what a jerk you are, you know. But geesh, TJ, you are just so really kindhearted sometimes." Rachel put her arms around his neck and kissed him thoroughly.

"Hmmm—" he murmured as he returned her affection.

She pulled away slightly and smiled at him. "Pretty good—for a dork, anyway."

"A dork? Really? I must be improving. I thought I was an asshole." He kissed her again. Rachel leaned in to him.

"Yeah, that too." She kissed his neck. "But you have managed to keep that promise—" She was totally serious now. "—and I just wanted to tell you how good a man you are to me."

"Thanks, Babe. I love you. And I will never stop being in love with you."

CHAPTER 19
If I Died Today

Once TJ and Rachel got back from their anniversary trip, Thanksgiving was right around the corner. Since the families usually shared part of their holidays together, the Metcafes joined the Keytons at the farm on Sunday afternoon before Thanksgiving. Rachel and Tina needed to make plans and confer about the menu. TJ, Mike and Ben took the four-wheelers to the fishing hole near the back of the property.

Though the weather was turning cooler, this happened to be one of those rare, perfect late autumn days. And the guys rarely passed up an opportunity to do a little fishing after church on Sundays.

Tina and Rachel, sweatshirts on, sat on the deck enjoying the shifting colors of the sky as the sunset glowed above the mountains. It was cool enough that Rachel had also brought out a couple of cozy couch throws. She and Tina leaned back in the deck chairs and chatted happily, sharing stories about their grandkids and making plans for the upcoming holidays.

Counting heads to decide how much food to prepare, Tina asked, "Will all the kids be around the Thanksgiving table this year?"

"I believe so. But for Christmas it will be hit and miss. We are taking the boys to Colorado to see Naomi and Erik and the twins the day after Christmas. Emily is doing a bunch of Christmas and New Year shows this year, and Mary is talking about hitting the road with her through the holidays. What about you guys?"

"Annie is planning on coming for Christmas, but probably not Thanksgiving. She loves being away until the holidays hit, or her birthday, and then she gets homesick. She has a hard time realizing we all have lives here, too."

Rachel pulled the cover over her arms as the sun lowered and the air became chilly. The men had been gone a couple hours and were due back soon before dark. They had big plans to grill up steaks and shrimp to go along with the salads already made by Rachel and Tina. Corn on the cob was simmering.

The whirr of a four-wheeler coming up the path behind the house caused Rachel to shield her eyes and peer in that direction.

"Uh-oh. I wonder why Ben is tearing back here so fast," Rachel said. "Hope he isn't in some kind of trouble. If he isn't in trouble, he will be if he doesn't slow down."

Tina turned her head to look.

Chapter 19: If I Died Today

Rachel expected to hear the other four-wheelers coming too, but she saw only Ben's. He sped around to the other side of the house. Thinking he was either upset about something or had been sent home because of something that happened at the pond, Rachel was halfway to her feet when she heard his panicked voice calling her from inside the house.

Normally she would wait until the boy found her, but there was something in his desperate cry that had both her and Tina on their feet. They met him in the hall by the back door.

"Mama!" His face was white and Rachel felt her heart sink into her belly. Something was terribly wrong.

"What is it Ben?" She tried to sound calm, but panic was quickly taking over all other senses.

Ben grabbed her hand, pulling her out the door and motioning for Tina to also follow.

"Daddy said to call 911, but you need to go quick. Out to the pond. Now!"

"Ben, what is it? Who's hurt? Is it your dad?"

Ben shook his head, still leading the women out the door. "Mama, they were fishing. I was on the other side. I looked over when I heard Daddy yell at Uncle Mike. I saw Uncle Mike fall. I ran over, but I didn't see him. Daddy was yelling at me to go call 911 and to get you and Aunt Tina."

Rachel was already on the ATV. As Tina climbed on behind her Rachel saw that her face was ashen. She was shaking, but she held tightly to Rachel. Rachel looked back at Ben holding the phone. For a brief moment she wanted to send Tina on her way and make the call herself, but then Tina began sobbing, urging Rachel to go. With one last look at her son, she gunned the four-wheeler, heading back the way Ben had come moments earlier when all had been calm with the world.

Tina was whispering into Rachel's back. Rachel couldn't hear the words, but her grip was intense around Rachel's waist. Rachel took one hand off the handlebars and squeezed her friend's hand. "It'll be okay," she said to Tina, and then to herself, over and over. "It will be okay."

She returned her hand to the handle to steady the machine as she sped out over the familiar territory. It felt as if they would never get to the pond. Rachel tried not to think of what might be waiting for them.

The pond itself was not accessible to motor vehicles. Seeing the other four-wheelers along the side, Rachel hit the brake and both she and Tina jumped off to run up the narrow path to the pond.

Tina stopped Rachel just before they topped the ridge.

Chapter 19: If I Died Today

Rachel had never seen her friend so completely undone, her eyes wide with fear, sorrow written all over her face. Already she was crying, fearful of what the moment of truth would be for them.

"Rache, what am I gonna tell my girls?" she sobbed.

"Honey, don't talk like that. You don't know yet what's happened." But the aching dread inside Rachel told her what she already knew. And her best friend felt it, too. She squeezed Tina's hand. Then Tina raced up the hill ahead of her to TJ who was bent low over Mike, administering CPR to his fallen friend.

TJ glanced up at the women and asked about the emergency crew, then quickly went back to work on Mike before they could give an answer.

Rachel felt the fear hit her stomach hard. She was scared for Tina and Mike—for her husband, too. The look of determination on his face and the pain apparent in his eyes were too much for Rachel. She put her hand on his back. Tina looked over TJ's shoulder at her husband.

"Is he breathing?" Tina asked in a choked whisper.

TJ shook his head. "Not for maybe ten minutes now."

With those words, Rachel saw a calmness come over Tina. She touched TJ's arm. "Let him go, Troy."

TJ kept working, willing that by some miracle his best friend in this world would breathe. Rachel and Tina exchanged a quick glance over TJ's back.

"Troy, let him go." Tina commanded with quiet assurance.

Rachel knelt beside her husband and looked at Mike's grey face. Their friend was no longer with them. Tina pushed her way closer to Mike as Rachel eased TJ away from his efforts. Once near his body Tina fell over her husband with a sob that brought fresh tears to Rachel's eyes. She saw TJ, too, was choking to breathe through his tears.

They moved away from Tina, giving her space to be with Mike. Rachel leaned against her husband and cried, silently watching, unable to do anything other than be with Tina in this moment.

After a while Tina sat back and her friends moved close around her. The three of them clung to each other and let their tears fall freely. They spoke no words as they sat in the weeds and held one another.

Rachel's mind was taking her through all that Mike meant to her, to her husband, to the man he had been to his own family. This was the man who had held TJ through his darkest hours of sorrow after the death of his first wife, Kris. This man and his wife had comforted TJ's children and loved them, prayed for them and pulled them through

Chapter 19: If I Died Today

when they lost their mama. This was the man that always greeted his wife with tenderness and respect, kissing her with such passion each time he left or entered a room. This man stood for Christ, and through his prayers and words had played a huge part in Rachel's husband's faith and sense of family. This man had helped TJ and Rachel make crucial life decisions about their relationship and about their family. He was the one TJ counted on most for brotherly advice and fatherly wisdom.

As Rachel sat near her friend, her heart ached knowing Tina was facing the loss of her true soul mate. Tina had known Mike since she was a teenager. They hadn't dated or married until after Tina had left home and then returned three years later, hurt and broken and with Laney. Mike had stepped in quietly beside Tina, helped her push through the tough years as a struggling country music artist and was the only father Laney had ever known. Tina and Mike had shared over twenty-five years of marriage.

All these thoughts and emotions crowded Rachel's mind. Her body felt numb. It seemed like hours the three of them sat there. Finally, the emergency response team crested the hill with Ben leading the way.

TJ moved forward to talk to the paramedics while Rachel and Tina stood close together, arms wrapped tightly around each other like sisters. Ben headed straight to the two women and they enfolded him in their embrace. He didn't normally like to be held, but for a moment he let himself be comforted. Rachel felt him shaking as he cried and clung to Aunt Tina and his mama, no longer the tough fourteen-year-old, but once again the small boy, broken by an unexpected tragedy.

Rachel touched his hair comfortingly then whispered in his ear, "You did good, angel-boy. It's going to be okay."

There wasn't anything about the situation that was okay. Not for any of them. In that moment, however, she wanted Ben to believe even though they were all sad they were going to make it through.

She didn't know how he would process this day. He had played a crucial role, an adult role, alerting her and Tina and calling the EMTs. She hoped it would help him to know he had been a strong man and a vital part of the family. Right now, all she could do was hold him and give him a soft place to let the tears and grief fall.

CHAPTER 20
If We Ever Needed You

After the coroner had arrived and Mike had been taken away for a routine autopsy, the group made their way back to the four-wheelers. They were told there was no need for them to follow Mike to the funeral home. They would be called later.

TJ and Ben headed out first. As he was leaving, TJ told Rachel quietly to take as much time as she needed with Tina. Rachel drove the four-wheeler slowly. Tina gripped Rachel's middle tightly. Tears kept blurring her own vision, and more than once she could feel Tina's sobs behind her.

Rachel knew the next few hours would be demanding as they would be making calls to let the family know. Only Mary and Ricky were home, but Rachel imagined the house would be full before the night was through. Those that lived close by would be over as soon as they could. Rachel pressed on, driving carefully and wondering what the evening would be like. She prayed for the grace to help her friend get through it.

"Rache, stop, will ya?" she heard Tina say.

Rachel pulled over. She turned off the engine and they both sat still. Finally, Tina gasped with a loud sob, "Oh Rache, I just don't know how I am going to tell those girls their precious daddy is gone!"

Rachel turned toward her friend. Her compassion for Tina ached so deeply she could hardly breathe. Shaking her head and touching her friend's face, she whispered, "I am so sorry. Honestly, I don't know." She paused a moment before she could continue. "But I will be right there with you."

Tina nodded. A fresh batch of tears coursed down her face. Rachel sat and allowed her friend the space and time to cry. Soon enough the family would gather and Tina would be hard-pressed on all sides by people that needed her. Rachel knew her friend well enough to know she would be strong for her children. Even in her own pain, she would be compelled to give comfort and support. There would be decisions to make. Rachel knew Tina needed this moment to fall apart without thoughts of being anything to anyone else. She felt no need to say anything. Rachel just held onto Tina and both women let their tears flow.

Finally, Tina wiped her tears and gave a forced laugh. "Mike wouldn't like all this carrying on, that's for sure."

Rachel chuckled quietly.

Tina continued. "But we went through all the other

Chapter 20: If We Ever Needed You

deaths—parents, Kris, other friends—together. I don't know what he was thinking leaving me like this." She wiped her eyes with her hand, but her nose was running, too. "Look at me," Tina laughed. "I am a giant weeping mess."

Rachel disagreed. Her friend was beautiful even while coming undone. Rachel gave her a weak smile and offered her sleeve as a tissue.

Tina shook her head and used her own sleeve. She sat up a little straighter as if to muster her resolve. "Okay. We better go, Rachel. Your family will be worried sick."

Rachel told her it was fine and to take her time, but Tina was ready.

"Gotta do the next step. Mike's always telling me when I don't like something, the only way through it, is through it. That's what it is, Rache. I just have to take one step at a time." She tried again to smile but it was weak and tears once more threatened to take over.

Rachel touched her arm. "I'll be here, Tina, and so will TJ. And you don't have to be tough for us. It's safe."

Tina squeezed Rachel's hand in affirmation. "Better get me back to the house. I have to get through these next few hours of talking to people." She resolutely drew in a deep breath and let it out slowly.

"Okay, then." Rachel turned on the machine and they

217

continued toward the house.

They found Mary, Rick and Ben in the front room with TJ. Ricky and Mary looked up with tears rolling down their cheeks. They got up quickly, joined Tina and Rachel in a desperate embrace.

Rick asked Tina if she was okay. Tina just shook her head. Ricky hugged her again. Rachel looked over at Ben, and he looked back at her, his eyes filled with tears, but he stayed seated and didn't join in the embrace. Rachel remembered he had allowed himself to be held and comforted out by the pond and was astounded at how well he had handled this crisis. When the others backed away Ben went to Tina and asked her if she wanted to sit down.

As Rachel watched her kids, she realized how tough the loss of Uncle Mike was going to be on them. He had been a huge influence in their lives, giving them another strong and stable male role model that loved them wholeheartedly and believed in them. Mike had often reinforced the values TJ and Rachel taught. He had welcomed Rachel's girls into the family with open arms. For Mike, the boys had been like the sons he never had. He let them know all the time how much they mattered to him. Rachel hurt for her children and prayed for wisdom and strength to help them through this.

Tina didn't sit. Instead she pulled Ben close to her. He

Chapter 20: If We Ever Needed You

responded to her hug and Rachel watched as fresh tears fell for all of them. This time Ben's embrace was to comfort his Aunt Tina whom he had admired and loved since the first time he met her when he was six years old. Tina thanked him when he told her he was sorry about Uncle Mike. She wiped a tear from his face and gently kissed his cheek. "We are going to make it through this, Baby," she told him.

TJ came to Rachel and put his arm around her. She rested her head on his chest for a moment then she looked up at him. "How are you holding up, Babe?" she whispered.

He just shook his head. His eyes were distant and guarded. Rachel knew him well enough to know he was putting his emotions aside so he could be strong and offer stability to Tina and all of them. But pain and loss were etched on his face. Rachel could not remember ever seeing him in this kind of pain. She wondered if her eyes held such evident sorrow. Her chest ached.

Tina excused herself to make a few calls. Rachel knew this was going to be tough so she decided to stay close. As she was leaving to follow Tina, TJ told her he had already called Hope and Gracie. "I can call Beth, Naomi and Emily, too, if you want," he offered.

"Thank you," she whispered. "You know the kids will all start calling each other, so you better call them all before they hear it from their sisters." TJ agreed and took out his phone while Rachel went out to find Tina on the back porch.

Tina was holding her cell phone, but hadn't been able to dial yet. She was taking deep breaths, trying to regain her composure so she could call Laney. Rachel quietly stood by her while she hit the speed dial on her cell.

When Laney picked up, Tina said, "Laney?" and then she broke down.

Rachel could hear Laney frantically saying, "Mama, what's happened? What is it?"

Tina, unable to talk, handed the phone to Rachel, shaking her head and covered her mouth, too late to stifle a wailing sob.

"Laney, honey, this is Aunt Rachel. Your daddy collapsed out fishing today with Uncle TJ—"

"Oh no!" Laney cried. "Is he alright?"

Rachel could tell she knew already that he wasn't okay. There was that sound in her voice that she knew the truth, but needed someone to confirm it. Tina, sensing the question, gently took the phone from Rachel.

"No, Baby. He's gone," she told her daughter.

CHAPTER 21
I Won't Let Go

They had stayed up all night and into the early morning hours. Rachel, TJ and Tina had been contacting friends and family, letting people know about Mike's death. Somewhere in the midst of the tearful calls, family members started gathering at the farm. Laney and her family had arrived first, followed by Beth and Hope. Rachel knew that in a few days people would also be gathering at Mike and Tina's ranch. From time to time Tina mentioned going home, but somehow she couldn't seem to summon the energy to get into the car. Rachel told her not to worry about going to the ranch. Tina was grateful.

Food mysteriously arrived. Even though Rachel was more coherent than Tina, she didn't notice who brought it, nor did she eat any of it. Later she realized members of their large church must have arranged for the meals to be dropped off. One of the girls, or perhaps even TJ made a run out to Tina's place and brought back some personal items she had requested.

Rachel began to notice how tired she felt. Tina had stretched out on the couch for a moment and actually fallen asleep. Rachel covered her with a blanket and prayed for her. Tina was such a small person yet so full of life and spunk. This was the first time Rachel had ever seen her look so tiny and frail.

TJ wasn't in their room when Rachel went in to change clothes and brush her teeth. Earlier he had been visiting with the kids. As each of them came in he had been called upon to repeat the story of what had happened. He had given hugs and words of comfort. She was sure the certainty of Mike's death had not fully hit any of them yet.

The initial shock was starting to wear off. Rachel still felt numb but the pain of the loss was also present. A few times Rachel had caught a glimpse of TJ's face in a rare moment when he wasn't talking on the phone or hugging one of the kids, and she could see the grief etched in his features. Out of all of them, TJ seemed the most deeply affected. He had not only witnessed Mike's death, but had desperately tried to save him. Rachel was sure he was replaying the entire incident over and over in his mind. She prayed for a way to bring him some comfort.

Around midnight the boys and their brothers-in-law had gone downstairs to play pool. No one was going to sleep. They just wanted to hang out together. The young women sat in the media room, talking. Rachel would catch parts of conversations, sometimes about Mike or other family memories, sometimes about unrelated topics.

Chapter 21: I Won't Let Go

Rachel was thankful for the house full of family and that they all had each other. Even when they were shooting pool or poking fun at one another, it was just as much a part of helping each other as their tears. Rachel was especially glad to see Ricky and Ben as part of the family.

Throughout the night, TJ had been handling all the incoming calls. At first Tina had her phone with her and fielded some of her own calls. But once her brother had been reached and she had connected with Annie in Europe, TJ gently took the phone from her. "Let me take the calls for a while," he had said. Rachel knew TJ was anticipating calls from outside the family to start pouring in.

Tina gratefully surrendered the phone. "TJ," she said, "it doesn't seem that long ago Kris died and we were going through this with you." Another wave of tears overtook Tina. Rachel watched her two best friends in the world sharing their losses and grief in a way Rachel could not.

Rachel finished brushing her teeth and washing her tear-stained face. Then she went to look for TJ. The house was quiet. It seemed all the kids had found places to crash. TJ was alone, sitting on a stool at the kitchen counter, a cup of cold coffee in his hands, his head bent low.

She stood in the doorway and watched him for a moment, not sure whether she should disturb him. Rachel was hurting and her sadness about Mike was overwhelming, but seeing TJ and Tina in so much pain was almost more than she could bear. TJ had a presence about him, usually larger than life, but in this moment he looked small, lost in his grief. It was almost as if he wanted to blend into the room and disappear inside himself.

Rachel thought about leaving him there. She felt unsure, having never seen him like this. But she knew enough about grief and loss to understand he needed her presence even if she didn't have any words to offer. Her heart was racing and aching at the same time and her love overshadowed her fear for him as she moved in to offer what comfort and support she could. She stood beside him a moment then quietly pulled out the bar stool beside him.

He raised his head and noticed her, his eyes weary, red, and swollen. He tried to give her a smile, but it fell flat. She put her hand on his arm and shook her head at his attempt to smile or talk or offer anything at all.

"Shhh. It's okay." She gently rubbed his back. They sat in silence for a minute. Then she asked quietly, "Babe, do you want to go lay down with me for a little bit?" It was more a suggestion than a question.

TJ shook his head slightly and started to say no or that he needed to do something else. Rachel mentioned that it looked

Chapter 21: I Won't Let Go

like everyone had fallen asleep, including Tina. "Maybe we could just hold each other for a bit," she offered again.

He sighed then let go of the coffee cup and stood. Rachel took his hand and gently led him to their room. She didn't remember a time when she had ever seen him this fatigued, this worn down or this miserable. Rachel turned toward him, and without a word, unbuttoned his shirt and slipped it off. He stood a moment by the bed as if he didn't have the energy to do anything else. Rachel helped him slip off his jeans and sit on the bed in his boxers, undershirt and socks.

Rachel lay down and coaxed him to lay back into the pillows. Wordlessly, she wrapped her body around his back and pulled the covers over them. She tenderly kissed his neck, and whispered in his ear that she loved him.

Through all of it TJ didn't say a word. Rachel prayed for him silently, for their family and for Tina. Lying against his back, she felt him exhale. While she hoped he would be able to relax enough to sleep, her own mind remained active. She pondered what would happen in the next few days, worried about TJ, Tina and the kids. She tried to force herself to focus on TJ's steady breathing and the warmth of his body. Exhaustion soon overtook her.

CHAPTER 22
Highway Don't Care

When Rachel woke it had been a scant few hours of sleep. Still, TJ was not in the bed and the morning light streamed through the window. It was only 6:30 but today was going to be long. All previous plans for the next few days were lost to wherever Mike's death and funeral arrangements would take them. Helping Tina and comforting family and friends would supersede any previous plans.

The memories of the evening before came flooding back and with them more tears and sorrow. Rachel took a minute, sitting on the edge of her bed to breathe a quick prayer and compose herself. She could hear talking in the kitchen. She hurriedly pulled her robe over her jammies.

As Rachel came around the corner into the kitchen she saw TJ near the coffee pot, his back against the counter. Tina sat at the table, cell phone to her ear, explaining yesterday. Was it really just yesterday? Already it seemed like a couple of days at the very least. TJ watched Tina, his own sorrow and weariness evident. He was unshaven and his eyes were still red, making his face appear paler than Rachel had ever seen it.

Rachel sidled up close to him to get some coffee. "Mornin,' Baby" He gave her a quick hug, but Rachel stayed in his arms, leaning on him.

"How are you?" she asked.

He didn't respond. He just nestled his chin on her head.

Then he leaned down whispered in her ear, "Thanks for last night."

Her eyes watered again at the thought of what this loss would mean for all of them. She glanced at Tina. TJ looked, too. She had finished talking, her back to them, leaning against the granite countertop, head on her arms, shoulders shaking with sobs.

Both of them moved to hold her, one on each side. Tina looked up, tears running down her face. She was so tough and yet so fragile.

"TJ," she said between sobs, "I don't know how you did this, losing Kris. I just don't know if I am gonna be able to make it through without Mike."

Rachel watched her friend lean on TJ much as she had just moments before. "One day at a time," he whispered. Rachel put her hand on her friend's back and the three of them sat while the coffee grew cold.

Chapter 22: Highway Don't Care

Finally, Tina's phone rang and she pulled away to answer it. Rachel heard a booming male voice. "Hey, Tony," Tina said to her brother. She moved away from the table to talk with him. Before Tina left the room Rachel heard him say he and Jenna were on their way.

Rachel glanced at her husband. The lines around his eyes were more prominent than she'd ever noticed and she wondered if she, too, looked tired and old. Even in his pain, though, TJ had a resolve and peace about him beyond his own strength. She knew that strength would be the faith that saw them all through.

"Rache." TJ took her hand. "I love you."

"Oh, Hon. I love you, too."

They sat for a moment holding hands, not saying anything, each lost in thought. Rachel was trying to put pieces together about what they needed to do and what would happen next. She hadn't had enough sleep to think clearly and could feel waves of emotion near the surface. What normal things needed to be done? It was Monday, a school day.

It seemed to hit TJ, too. "Rachel, it's gonna get crazy here for the next week or so. What about school? What do we need to do to keep things somewhat sane for the boys?"

Keeping a routine had always been extremely important

for Ricky and Ben. Even though they were better than in the past at handling transitions and disruptions to normal life, both she and TJ knew that helping them through this intense emotional situation might hinge on keeping some things as consistent as possible.

"Well, it is Thanksgiving week, so school will be out a few days anyway. I will call the school and let them know what is going on. The boys don't really need to go to school today. They need the structure, but at the same time I feel certain they need to be here with everyone. Mike was a huge part of their lives and staying connected with family right now is important."

Rachel paused, thinking about Thanksgiving and the planned family gatherings. This was not going to be a normal Thanksgiving. She tried to imagine what it was going to be like for the boys. She looked up at TJ.

"I am just not sure when all the emotions and the loss of their Uncle Mike will hit them. I don't know how hard it will hit them or what it will look like for either one of them to grieve."

"Yeah," TJ agreed. "It might bump against a lot of other losses and be even more painful. Or with their defensiveness, they might just push it all aside."

Rachel loved that he got it.

Chapter 22: Highway Don't Care

"I'll try to stay close to them. We'll have to tag-team this. Tina is going to need us and so will the other kids."

Rachel clung to him. "We'll both be hurting and needed at the same time. Just check in with me from time to time, okay?"

TJ lifted her chin and kissed her tenderly in agreement. They pulled apart a little when Tina came back in the kitchen. She was shaking her head and laughing as she put her phone back in her pocket.

"No one can make me laugh like that crazy brother of mine," she said. "He and Jenna are on their way over." She gave a quick laugh. "What a goof-ball. Here I am crying about losing Mike and he teases me about marrying an older man."

Rachel chuckled along with her friend. Then Tina's face turned serious and her eyes teared up again as the magnitude of the loss hit her like a wave.

"Well," TJ said moving toward the door to the hall, "do we know what we have to do today?"

And that was how their days went. One minute laughter about something Mike had said or done, the next tears, hugs and surrendering to the loss. The place that was once Mike in their lives was a gaping hole. Rachel, Tina, TJ, Jenna and

Tony answered phone calls, fielded questions, and along with Laney, planned the funeral. Days and nights blurred together. No one missed Thanksgiving dinner as people were constantly coming and going.

The first Monday, the day after Mike had died, Rachel had driven Tina over to the ranch as Tina had requested. Once there, Tina said she just couldn't be there alone yet. She didn't get out of the car. Rachel and Beth quickly gathered some more of her things. She stayed with the Keytons for the remainder of the week.

Although the Metcafes had plenty of caretakers at their ranch TJ went over several times to make sure things were being handled and had tighter security put in place. He also dealt with the press and shielded Tina and Laney as much as he could. Mail came in by the bucket load from adoring fans offering their sympathy. TJ, having gone through his wife's death at the height of his career, understood how to deal with the public. He told Rachel that Mike had handled so much of it he hardly remembered talking to anyone the first year after Kris's death. He felt the least he could do was to protect Tina in the same way.

Even though Tina was retired, she was still a celebrity. While they usually experienced very little pressure from the media in their little town near Nashville, now camera crews, reporters and fans seemed to be everywhere they

Chapter 22: Highway Don't Care

turned. Mike was well-known and well-loved by almost as many people in the business as Tina. TJ did his best to get people on duty to protect the family's privacy and yet deal sensitively with the media.

It wore on Rachel and the kids who were asked questions anytime they left the farm or answered their phones. They tried to stay close to home and close to each other. Because leaving the farm was becoming more and more difficult, friends from church brought food and anything else they needed to them.

TJ, always a master with public relations, helped Tina make one press appearance. When he got too cautious and tried to keep anyone from bothering her with sympathies or wanting to gain information, it was Tina that reminded him people just cared and wanted her to know they were sending love. Nonetheless, TJ insisted on security at the ranch as well as their farm.

With all the people around, decisions to be made and various issues to be fielded, TJ acted and reacted as he usually did. He stepped in and handled details like a pro. Tina and her family leaned on him. He was solid as a rock. But at the end of the day and in the early morning hours when he couldn't sleep Rachel would find him alone in the kitchen or downstairs in his office. Much like he had been the first night, he often stared blankly at the computer screen or off into the distance. At those times Rachel could see his own grief pressing on him.

Sometimes she would wake, find his side of the bed empty and seek him out. Other times long after everyone else had gone to bed she would go find him and sit with him. They didn't talk much, but she would rub his back or hold his hand. She did what she could to offer her strength and her support. He needed someone to lean on and she tried to lend herself to him.

TJ was tough and when he was upset he coped by getting stronger. Mike had been someone who broke through TJ's defenses. So Rachel tried to provide times when he didn't have to be strong or provide answers. He would allow her to hold him and more often than not he would tell her what he was thinking or feeling.

In those quiet moments he would tell her how this all felt so similar to when Kris had died and how powerless he felt then and now. He lamented he had not been able to do anything to save Mike. Rachel listened as he went over and over the details of that Sunday afternoon. It seemed as though he was talking to himself, trying to convince himself he had done all he could to save his best friend. Through all of it Rachel listened and comforted, and mostly she prayed. The pain she saw in him was bigger and deeper than anything she could touch or heal.

Chapter 22: Highway Don't Care

Most nights she would coax him to bed. And when he finally drifted off, she would find her own sorrow hitting her. It wasn't as though she carried it alone, because during the day she found comfort in her connection with her family and with Tina. They grieved openly together.

It was TJ she worried about. Even Ben and Ricky were doing better at truly engaging and being comforted with the others. While it was difficult to watch her husband and Tina carry so much pain, Rachel realized TJ was pulling inward in a way she had never seen. Once everyone went back home and life started to return to normal, what would TJ do with his own heartache?

With daytime activities, people calling and family in and out, Rachel would find TJ mingling with the kids or talking with Tina. He was clearly the head of the family. Sometimes she would wonder if the brokenness she saw in him at nights was real or her imagination. But then TJ would catch her in a quiet moment and thank her for being with him the night before. Hard as it was, Rachel was thankful she had those moments with him. She felt he trusted her and Rachel found it meant the world to her.

CHAPTER 23
From Ricky's Journal

My Uncle Mike and Aunt Tina are the coolest people you can imagine. Aunt Tina is this great singer and sometimes she would take Ben or me with her backstage before her concerts. She is not my mom's real sister, but I guess she and my dad are such good friends that they all call each other family.

When we were little we thought it was so much fun to follow Uncle Mike around his ranch and help him do chores. I am sure we weren't much help, but he always acted like we were really tough little cowboys mucking out stalls and helping him carry bales of hay. We have the same kind of chores at our own farm, but there was something about doing it with Uncle Mike that made it seem different and fun. I think Uncle Mike was what I imagined having a grandpa would be like.

My mom and Aunt Tina are best friends and my sisters were the same way with Laney and Annie. Right from the start Ben and I were included in their family, too. Late nights *in the summer playing softball, swimming at their house or at ours and sleepovers when our parents were out of town were some of the best things I remember about being a little kid.*

I don't know what Aunt Tina is going to do without Uncle Mike. They were the kind of adults you could tell really liked being around each other. I mean, they were really close. My parents are like that, too, and I don't think my mama would want to live here without Daddy.

That day it happened was such a bad day. In the first place, I couldn't go fishing with them because I had some stupid paper I had to write for school. Of course, I had waited to do it until Sunday. I was actually really mad about it. So I was in a bad mood and trying to make myself write the stupid thing instead of going out with the guys.

I came downstairs to get something when I saw Mama and Aunt Tina go zooming away on the four-wheeler. I thought I heard Ben talking on the phone, kind of yelling. I couldn't figure out what was going on. I went into the kitchen when Ben was coming in from the patio with the phone in his hand. I thought I saw tears in his eyes.

I asked him what was going on. He said, "Uncle Mike is dead I think." Then he just dropped to his knees and started crying. I stood there for a minute not really registering what I was hearing or what I was seeing.

Chapter 23: From Ricky's Journal

You have to understand, my big brother is tough. Ben and my daddy are both tough in the same way. They always seem to be strong even when things are really bad. I just got down on the floor and sat there with him. I think I was crying, too. He told me between sobs about how he heard Daddy yell Uncle Mike's name, how he ran over while Dad started CPR. Daddy hollered at him to go home, get Aunt Tina and call 911. I remember feeling really scared when Ben told me that.

We sat there on the kitchen floor, me and Ben, for a long time. When my brother was telling me about racing home to call 911, I thought about how Ben and daddy just sprang into action. Sometimes their actions are all wrong and angry, but they always do something. I freeze up when I'm scared, but they are fighters.

How in the world was my brother able to make that call to the emergency services, give directions and still manage to get Mama and Aunt Tina on their way? How was my daddy calm enough to try to save Uncle Mike's life?

I remember praying when I was on the floor with Ben that maybe Daddy did save Uncle Mike. I knew if I had been out there with them fishing I would have been standing there just watching Daddy, unable to think or move. For the first and last time, I was glad I had that paper to do.

Here's what I said to Ben when he was crying. "You don't know if he is dead for sure." *Which, that was probably pretty dumb to say but I wanted Ben to be wrong.*

"Rick—" Ben looked at me with red eyes and his really somber expression. *"—Dude, he already didn't even look like Uncle Mike. I don't think he was alive even when Daddy got there and started CPR."* He shook his head at the memory. *"I never saw a dead guy before."*

We sat there a long time, not really saying anything, just waiting for the adults to come home. Then Mary was the one that came in. I remember because she came around the corner and saw us there. Her arms were full of stuff she was going to take out to her cottage. She always cheated and went through the house instead of around through the back gate like Daddy told her to do a million times.

She took one look at us and started freaking out. I remember her yelling, *"What happened?"* It's weird how you just know something really bad happened even without words. Ben told her about Uncle Mike, and Mary went all kind of hysterical. I might be frozen and not know what to do in a crisis, but Mary was just plain crazy. Thankfully, about that time was when Ben had to leave to take the rescue team

Chapter 23: From Ricky's Journal

out to the pond. She stopped freaking out when she saw Ben acting like an adult and dealing with the emergency crew.

By the time Daddy and Ben came back Mary was pretty quiet. Daddy came in and Mary saw the look on his face. We all knew. But Mary had another little melt-down. I couldn't say anything. I just kept thinking Ben had been right about Uncle Mike.

Daddy had us wait in the front room. He said Mama and Aunt Tina were coming back from the pond soon. So we were kind of sitting quietly. I remember Mary was crying and my face was wet with tears even though I didn't think I was crying. Daddy was holding onto Mary.

I was looking at my dad. What I remember was that he looked older. It was the worse I had ever seen him. My daddy is my rock. And just like Uncle Mike, he loves life and he brings life with him in everything he does. I guess I am still young enough to believe he never fails at anything. Daddy always has this superhero quality about him, at least to me.

Seeing him that day, he looked smaller and more human. I wanted to comfort him, but at the same time I wanted him to be strong and comfort me. So I just sat across the room, and hoped Mama would be home soon, because I guess I felt like she would know what to do, especially about Daddy.

As a little kid, before I came to live here, there were never any people I remember really taking care of Ben and me. Mostly what I remember is Ben. I have some vague recollection of our birth mother and a few foster homes. I don't remember having a daddy or an uncle or a family for that matter. There was no one to lose. But then again, Mama says we had so much loss that we couldn't understand what it meant to really have someone. I don't know. I just know Uncle Mike being dead is not something any of us are going to get over anytime soon.

It's been almost two weeks now and everyone else is going back to their lives—to work or to their own houses. We are going to have to go back to school. I think Emily is getting ready to leave on tour again. My cousins and sisters are not going to be the same without Uncle Mike. But my Aunt Tina, Mama, and Daddy, they are the ones I worry about.

Bad stuff happens to kids a lot, but there are usually adults to help somehow. I'm not sure what kids are supposed to do when the adults are going through so much. I am not sure how we are going to go back to regular life, one without Uncle Mike in it. So what are we supposed to do?

CHAPTER 24
Cry, Cry (Till the Sun Shines)

In the days before the funeral Tina seemed to get stronger. Her grief and sorrow were still raw, but through it all, Rachel saw Tina's inner strength. She had always been a resilient woman and Rachel respected how, despite her own pain, she was able to bring comfort to those around her. She didn't hide her sorrow, nor did she shrink from it. She was transparent, unafraid to be vulnerable. In sharing her grief openly she allowed those around her to be open and vulnerable as well.

Rachel was with her as Tina faced multiple decisions, talked to family members and dealt with her fans. Rachel couldn't help but admire her friend and she knew Mike would have been proud of her poise at such a difficult time. Even during such a trying time, Tina was someone others, including Rachel, could draw strength from.

Sometimes laughing through tears, other times wrestling through sobs, Tina faced managing day-to-day life without Mike with grace and dignity. She wasn't afraid to share her heartache and even her anger. Her honesty and strength of character spoke volumes about her faith and her love for Mike. Being there with her, Rachel felt better able to express her own loss. Being near Tina helped Rachel when she needed to help TJ and the kids through the struggles and waves of emotion.

When Annie arrived from London late in the week she wanted to hear in detail what had happened. It was good for Tina to have her girls with her. She pulled away from the people milling around the house to spend time with her daughters. It was the first Rachel saw of hope for what Tina would have in her life that was solid and sure when she moved on without Mike. Tina leaned on her friends and family and pulled her girls in close.

By Thursday, Rachel found she was completely exhausted. As much as she wanted to be there for her friend, she was beginning to wish for some sort of normalcy. Then she would feel horrible for wanting everyone to go home. She realized for Tina normal was over for a long time.

Even though she was tired, Rachel was thankful for how everyone was supporting each other and preoccupied with family. The boys had been busy all week with their cousins, nieces, nephews, and siblings. Rachel knew sometime in the near future she would need time with her kids to help them process all that had happened, but for the moment, kids being kids, they were engaged with all the family and only mildly concerned about the sadness.

Chapter 24: *Cry, Cry (Till the Sun Shines)*

There was a private family viewing the Friday after Thanksgiving. Rachel was occupied helping Tina, Laney and Annie finalize plans for the funeral on Saturday. That morning Tina had said she was ready to go home. She said she wanted time there before the funeral and time with her girls at home so it wouldn't all be over at the same time.

"It will just be too much, Rache, if I go home for the first time after a final good-bye to Mike. I have to go home now so I can start getting used to it while I still have my family with me. Besides, you and TJ and your family need some space, too."

"Don't worry about us. Having you and the girls here has been a huge blessing. You don't even know how it has helped us all to go through it together as a family. But Tina, if you find out there are times you can't be there at the ranch, and you need to be around you can always come here—day or night."

"I know it, Sweetie." Tina gave Rachel a big hug. "And thanks. For everything from going to the ranch with me to get stuff we needed to housing us, hugging us and just everything. You too, TJ." She grabbed TJ in a big bear hug.

He held on to her and echoed Rachel's words. "You come over anytime you need to, Tina. You know I sure visited you all a lot after Kris. Or call us, anytime, day or night." He made her promise she would. And just like that, she, Laney, Annie, Tony and Jenna plus all the Metcafe extended family members were gone.

It wasn't a large group that exited, especially compared to how many people were still milling about the house, but it still felt empty to Rachel. She tried to imagine what the ranch was going to feel like to Tina without Mike there. It was too painful to consider at the moment. Rachel hoped and prayed Tina would take them up on the offer to come and go as often as needed.

The day of the funeral it was cold. The wind blew with all its winter bitterness. It was almost a relief to know the funeral and all the planning would be over after this day. Rachel knew she and TJ needed to get to the auditorium early. She hurried to get ready for the day.

Ben and Ricky had never been to a funeral. They had been too young to remember much from when TJ's dad died. Neither of them were old enough or mature enough to witness the open casket or be part of the emotional trial of that particular situation. But Mike was someone they had been especially close to. And even though Ben had already expressed that he did not want to go, TJ and Rachel wanted the boys to be there today.

Yesterday they had gone with Rachel to the viewing time

Chapter 24: *Cry, Cry (Till the Sun Shines)*

to say good-bye to their Uncle Mike. Ben had refused to step beyond the doorway and Rick had lingered there with his brother. Finally, Rick had made his way to Mike's side. Tears rushed down his cheeks. Rachel stood behind him with her hand on his shoulder, in tears herself, while he took a long look at this beloved friend.

"Uncle Mike," she heard Ricky say in a small voice, "I already miss you."

Rick leaned against Rachel and she wrapped her arms around him. "I miss him too," she said.

"We won't ever forget him, will we?" he said. Rachel thought about all the loss this boy had had in his young life, even those he had no real memory of—grandparents, aunts, uncles, mother and father.

"No, we never will. And we will be telling Uncle Mike stories forever, I think." She smiled to herself. She held Rick for a while, both of them silent. Finally he pulled away a little.

Rachel looked back at Ben. He had moved in a little closer, but not within her reach.

"Ben, Hon, do you want to come over and say good-bye to Uncle Mike?"

He shook his head and backed up to the door again. Rachel

took a deep breath and slowly exhaled. It was the hardest thing to reach out to Ben sometimes. She didn't know if she should pull him in or let him push away.

Right then, behind Ben, Tina came in with TJ. They had been talking to the funeral home staff about the arrangements for the next day. TJ put his hand on Ben's shoulder and sort of guided him in a few steps. It surprised Ben, Rachel could tell, because it took him a couple steps before he tensed up and froze. TJ stopped with him.

Tina came over to Rachel and Rick. She looked at the tears still fresh on their faces and her eyes teared up, too. Rachel and Rick both moved to embrace her. She held onto Ricky and motioned with her head toward Ben.

TJ and Ben had found seats in the back of the viewing room. Rachel silently lowered herself into the chair on the other side of Ben. TJ still had his hand on Ben's shoulder. It was as close to a hug as Ben probably would allow. TJ looked at Rachel and shook his head slightly to indicate he wasn't going to get Ben any closer.

Rachel patted Ben's knee. "Son. I am not sure what this is like for you. I can guess it is really hard. You don't have to go up there to see him. It might be better if you don't. If you want to be alone we can let you have some time in the room to say good-bye or if you want us to go with you closer

Chapter 24: *Cry, Cry (Till the Sun Shines)*

we can. Or we can just stay back here. It's okay. This time is for you."

Ben didn't say anything. He moved his knee away from Rachel's hand and sat still with his body hunched forward. TJ looked over Ben's head at Rachel with compassion. It was always tough emotionally when Ben chose to distance himself. Rachel shrugged a little and they sat together silently.

Rick came over and said he was going to the washroom. Rachel quietly told him where it was. Ben still had not spoken. TJ draped his arm over Ben's chair to touch Rachel's arm. They simply waited out the moment. Finally, Ben moved and slowly stood.

He didn't look at them at all. He shoved his hands into his pockets and walked over to Tina. She greeted him with a big hug and Ben accepted her embrace. Rachel watched as he stood with Tina and leaned against her. Tina told him something and he gave her a dim smile. She squeezed his arm and then she turned and sat in Ben's seat between TJ and Rachel.

"He wanted to say something to Mike alone," Tina whispered. Rachel nodded. And the three adults watched Ben for a moment longer. He didn't stay long. When he was done, he turned away and walked past the small group of adults without so much as a glance in their direction.

"Okay," TJ said as he stood. "Tina, do you need to stay a little longer?" He pointed to the boys hanging back in the hallway. "I can go on home with the guys if you don't need me to give you a ride back to the ranch."

"I will catch a ride with the girls later. Or Tony and Jenna are coming by shortly and I can go with them. I will probably be here a while more." She looked at Rachel, sadness overtaking her. Tina whispered, her lips trembling. "I know I have to say good-bye for the last time, too. But not quite yet."

Rachel nodded and gave her friend a squeeze. "Stay as long as you need to, Sweetie."

Rachel was glad Ben's few moments with Tina had allowed him to be brave enough to say good-bye to Mike. On the way home Ben was quiet. Rachel didn't push for him to share. Hard as it was at times to watch him give affection or open up with someone else more than herself, Rachel was thankful he loved Tina. He would do just about anything for her.

Now, turning away from thoughts of the last days' events, Rachel headed upstairs to see if the boys were ready for the funeral. She knocked on Ben's door first and heard him mutter something. She peered in. He was sitting on his bed

Chapter 24: Cry, Cry (Till the Sun Shines)

wearing sweatpants, a baseball cap and his football practice jersey. His nice clothes had been shoved onto the floor and he didn't look like he was planning on getting ready anytime soon.

"Ben?" Rachel looked at him questioningly. "You don't look ready to go."

"Not going," he said matter-of-factly.

"Hmm. My understanding was we were all going together today."

"Well," Ben looked at her coldly. "I don't want to. That's all. Can you understand that?"

He sounded angry, almost snarling. Rachel knew if she pushed hard now it would be a full battle. She paused, praying silently. Then she sat next to him. He scooted away from her to the other side of the bed. She waited. Nothing was said for several minutes. Ben fiddled with a trinket he had in his hand.

"Are you going to make me go?" His tone was softer, although Rachel could still sense his defensiveness.

She studied him. He was scrunched against the headboard. Tall as he was, he looked young.

"I don't know," she said kindly. She took deep breaths

and tried not to think about how to make him come or how late they might be if he had a full-scale blow up.

"No one really ever wants to go to a funeral," she added. "So, you know, it's not like I blame you or anything for not wanting to go."

He lifted his head and seemed to uncurl from the tight ball he had been in. He looked at his hands and not at her. "It was weird seeing Uncle Mike like that last night," he said.

Rachel agreed. She didn't want to say too much. She was glad Ben had started to open up. He glanced over at her. She looked into his eyes which were starting to water a little. Then he looked away and brushed a hand roughly across his face.

"Yeah, well. I don't want to go. I saw him. I said goodbye. It's just stupid."

"Okay," she nodded. "I would like everyone to be there. Naomi got in late last night and so all your sisters will be there. Our family was very special to Mike, and still is to Tina. Your sisters lost their mom before I married your dad, and Mike and Tina, Laney and Annie helped them get through it. And this is really hard for your dad too. I know it is hard for you. I don't know how to get through hard stuff like this without us sticking together."

Chapter 24: Cry, Cry (Till the Sun Shines)

Ben didn't say anything. He stretched out his legs and looked up. She followed his gaze around the room. He sighed heavily and then went back to looking at his hands.

"Is there anything that would make it easier for you to go?"

He shrugged. Rachel waited. She didn't want to push him to the point of feeling like he had no option but to defy her or give in completely. So she just gave him time. Thoughts of things she could say or do rushed in her mind, but she forced herself to stay quiet and calm and hope for the best.

It felt like an hour, but in truth it had been only a few minutes when Ben said, "Fine. I'll go." He was definite and defiant. "But I am not wearing those clothes." He pointed to the blue, button-down shirt, tie, and black dress pants.

"Fine," she said firmly. "Fair enough. But you can't wear that." She pointed to the outfit he was wearing. She stood to leave.

"Aren't you going to tell me what to wear?" he asked.

"I think you can find something that will work." She wanted to remind him it should meet his dad's approval, but she stopped herself. She could have urged him to keep in mind they were going to be in front of a large crowd, including lots of media. Instead, she prayed silently and said encouragingly, "If you want help with it let me know. But I think you got this."

After she had checked on Ricky, she told the boys to be downstairs in fifteen minutes. They needed to arrive early since she and TJ were helping with the service. It was going to be held at the Ryman in Nashville. A large crowd was expected as Mike and Tina had many friends.

Rick was the first downstairs. He was dressed in black slacks and a red button-down shirt. He had a tie in his hand. Rachel brushed his hair out of his eyes with her hand and then she hugged him. He told her he wanted to wear the red shirt because it was Uncle Mike's favorite color. His eyes held traces of tears.

TJ saw the tie and motioned Ricky over. Rachel watched TJ tease Ricky about not passing the ninth grade until he could tie his own tie. While they were finishing up, TJ happened to look up from fixing Ricky's collar and noticed Ben coming down the stairs. Smiles vanished.

"Oh no. You go on back up and put on the clothes your mother picked out," TJ said. He pointed at Ben's jeans and old football jersey. Ben stood still on the bottom step. He looked at Rachel, pleading. TJ followed the look and turned to Rachel. "Did you tell him he didn't have to dress up?"

Rachel nodded. TJ clenched his jaw. He was immediately

Chapter 24: Cry, Cry (Till the Sun Shines)

annoyed. "Rachel, what? You know we are going to be up in front, media, the whole bit. Why do let him do whatever he wants?" He threw his hands up. "I can't believe this."

Rachel looked from TJ to Ben. Ricky had moved closer to his brother. They presented a more united front than she and TJ at the moment. She hadn't had a moment to talk to TJ about Ben and what he was going through. She had hoped to support TJ by making sure everyone got there in one piece without too much hassle.

She wondered what would be best. Ben was great at getting them to play against each other. Rachel had to be careful because he excelled in dividing and conquering when he needed power or control. If it looked like she was siding with Ben and making TJ change his mind she would pay for it later. It was tricky, but she moved closer to TJ in a way that not only kept things from escalating with Ben, but also showed her unity with TJ.

"Babe, I didn't tell him he could wear whatever he wanted." Rachel caught his eye as she continued. "He knew he would have to meet with your approval in what he decided to wear. But I made the suit optional because he needed a compromise. I figured him going was even more important than what he wore."

"Well, this isn't going to cut it." Turning to Ben TJ told

him to go back upstairs and change clothes. "—into the ones your mama picked out for you."

"I'm not going then," Ben said stubbornly. "It's bad enough we have to go to this stupid thing with all these people that didn't even know Uncle Mike and then we can't even wear our normal stuff." "I hate this! I am not going!"

TJ gave Ben a long, hard look. Like two bulls, they locked eyes. Then Rachel heard TJ breathe in deeply. He rubbed his chin, a sure sign he was trying to stay calm. Rachel silently prayed. The last thing any of them needed was a power struggle right now. Ben was setting the stage perfectly for one. She also knew from experience jumping in the middle would end badly. She had to wait it out.

"Ben, we don't have time for this," TJ gave an exasperated gesture. "I really need you to simply do what you are told today."

Ben stood his ground and glared at his dad.

TJ finally turned to Rachel. "Okay. What? You're the counselor. What do I do?"

Rachel shrugged and said, "It's up to you two." She did her best to seem indifferent and yet supportive. "Maybe you guys can come to a compromise?" She motioned for Ben to come closer. Thankfully Ben took a few steps.

Chapter 24: Cry, Cry (Till the Sun Shines)

Compromise was code for when both sides needed to give and share power. The boys had been taught to ask for a compromise when they were young. It helped them express what they wanted or needed. It had been one of the best tools in softening the absolutes and ultimatums that power struggles produced.

TJ caught her meaning. She stepped back to let them work it out. It just might work if they could both say what they wanted to happen and come to an agreement.

"Son, this is a hard day for me." As far as Rachel knew, TJ hadn't spoken to the kids about the funeral before. He told Ben he was nervous, and that he felt uptight trying to do things right today for Tina and Mike's family. Rachel could see Ben softening in light of his dad's honesty. TJ's voice choked as he talked about how hard it was to lose his friend.

"It may seem to you like I am not too sad. But it is because I am busy trying to help Aunt Tina. All I want to do today is provide everyone coming a chance to pay respect to your Uncle Mike and to Aunt Tina. Maybe you think I don't care how hard this day is for you and our family, but I know it is. It's hard for me, too, and I need you all here with me today. It is important to me that I can sit next to you boys and your sisters. I want you with me because we are all going to miss Uncle Mike. It may seem stupid to you, this funeral, but this is a chance for everyone outside our family to also hear about and remember what a great guy Uncle Mike was."

He lowered his head and put his hand on the back of his head as if searching for words. "Honestly, Ben, you being next to me right now means more to me than what you wear. So if I have to choose between you being there not dressed up or you not being there at all, I choose you to be with me."

Rachel had tears running down her face. She waited as Ben seemed to weigh and measure his dad's words. He was looking down but when he looked up at TJ his face was tear streaked, too. He shifted from one foot to the other.

"Daddy, I wanted to wear the clothes that remind me of being around Uncle Mike. My football jersey reminds me of him coming to my games and all the times we played at the ranch. Uncle Mike was easy to be around and I just wanted to feel comfortable today like when he was here."

TJ stepped close to Ben and put his arm around his shoulder. Nearly nose to nose, he said, "Okay, Son. I get it."

Minutes later Rachel, TJ, Mary and the boys got into the car, Ben in his nice suit pants, shirt and tie with his football jersey pulled over them.

CHAPTER 25
He Didn't Have to Be

Rachel had never been to a funeral this large for anyone she knew. In retrospect, she realized she had not been around many funerals at all. They had buried TJ's dad, Tim, at a small graveside service with only their immediate family. Before she met TJ her own father had died and she had helped with his funeral, also a small family affair. She had seen large televised funerals of movie stars or recording artists. She had never imagined being part of one of those.

When Kris died TJ had been at the height of his career so her funeral had been big news. Tina had once shown Rachel parts of the recorded event. The family grieved in small, quiet pockets, but the media fed on the public sympathy and fanfare. With Kris, and now Mike, thousands paid tribute to the spouse of someone they loved dearly.

Mike, although not a famous artist, was not a quiet, reserved man. He made friends wherever he went. While Tina was on stage he was usually meeting everyone from showground janitors to up-and-coming performers. He knew stagehands and producers. Often before shows it was Mike choosing fans to meet Tina personally backstage. He never sang with Tina, but he was at just about every event or show she ever did. Tina would joke that they would go to breakfast in some small, obscure town while touring and no matter where they were someone would know Mike and come over to talk. He was just that kind of guy.

Sometimes you don't realize how much a person's life touches others until that person dies. Letters had been pouring in from Tina's fans, but most were people Mike had influenced, helped or inspired. Mike was solid as a rock. His life as a friend, a father, an uncle, and a husband meant the world to his family and those close to him. But in his death Rachel learned how much he had impacted the larger world around him.

He held out his faith as a light for others. Many found their way because of Mike. He was the kind of person who would take the time to talk to everyone. He would ask the wait staff at restaurants about their day or their kids. He knew people by their first names or by nicknames he had affectionately bestowed on them.

When they toured Tina would stay in the bus before a show, but Mike would be talking to people right up until they hit the road for the next town. He literally knew everyone on the crew in small towns and big cities all over the country. Many times they would be late to dinner or to hit the road after a show because Mike was praying with the guy in the

Chapter 25: He Didn't Have to Be

t-shirt booth or be praying with a janitor at the event center because the poor man had just learned his wife had cancer. Mike prayed with countless people through the years.

At the funeral several people attested to the fact that it was Mike's steadfast love for God and people that had profoundly impacted those around him. TJ spoke about how Mike had influenced him when he was "young and stupid," starting to make it big, but running with a wild crowd. Mike had the courage to confront TJ when he was hell-bent on making wrong choices and hurting those closest to him.

"Mike wouldn't let me just go my own way. He told me he cared too much to let me misuse my gifts. And it was my best friend Mike that lead me right back to my childhood faith and showed me a real relationship with Jesus Christ."

Later, at Tina's request, Rachel shared about Mike's gentle wisdom and kindness to her and how he had welcomed her family into his own family. She gave him honor for the role model he had been to her sons and daughters. "Mike hated good-byes," she said. "He would just give you a hug and say, 'See ya later.'"

Although many touching sentiments had been spoken by friends and family, Rachel was sure not a dry eye remained while Laney spoke. Laney stood before the crowd of thousands near the end of the service to pay tribute to the man who had been the only father she had ever known. She talked about being a little girl when she met him and how she looked up to him. She said she was completely convinced at five years old that he had married her mom just so he could be her daddy.

Rachel knew she would never forget Laney saying, "Some kids grow up hating God because He is called a Father. They don't know what a great father is like. My daddy wanted everyone without a father to know the kind of daddy God really is. But the best thing for me and my sister Annie was that our daddy lived his faith in our home and with us. He loved God, he loved my sister and me, and we always knew he loved our mama. Some men get in the way of their children seeing Jesus or seeing the heart of God. Our daddy gave us, every day, real understanding of love and family. He made it easy for us to understand God as our Father."

All throughout the funeral, Emily sat between Rachel and Tina. Her tears never stopped. Even though Rachel could tell Emily had been drinking that day she seemed to soak in every word. Emily was overtaken by the testimony of Mike's life and the emotions of the day. Rachel prayed Mike's death would minister to others, even those in her family. When Emily stood up to leave with the others for the private graveside service, she first hugged Rachel and then the boys, but it was TJ she embraced the longest.

Chapter 25: He Didn't Have to Be

Rachel heard Emily say to him, "I'm sorry, Daddy." She was clinging to him. Rachel had to unwind her arms from him so he could help carry the casket with the other pallbearers. Then Emily leaned against Rachel and sobbed. "He was the daddy he didn't have to be." Rachel wasn't sure if Emily was talking about TJ or Mike.

CHAPTER 26
From Ricky's Journal

Ever since Uncle Mike died things have been pretty weird at my house. First of all, my brother, who is usually the one in trouble all the time, has been doing good—really good. He is actually making a few friends at school and he hasn't gotten in a fight since he quit football, which was actually even before Uncle Mike died.

Another weird thing is Emily has been home a lot more. And she has been more like her old self. She has been helping Mama at the house, giving Ben and me rides and even going to church with us. After Uncle Mike's funeral, she took time off the road, and she moved in with Beth. She told me she was still going to be a big country star, but she needed some time to "get her head together." Whatever that means. She's back though, and that makes me happy.

I like it best when my whole family is close by. This winter was a good winter to have my sister near us and my brother doing better. It's the best part of everything being so different and the best that has come from Uncle Mike's passing.

Even though all these good things have been happening there is some weird bad stuff, too. The biggest has to do with

Daddy, and the other has to do with me. I guess they are kind of connected. I know my dad misses Uncle Mike a lot. And since the funeral, he has not been the same at all. One of the highlights—or lowlights I guess—is he now gets irritated easily, and he always seems unavailable. What I mean is, he doesn't talk or even really seem to want to be around us anymore.

So like about a month ago one night at dinner I was right in the middle of telling everyone a story about this girl in my class. It was no big deal, really. Ben, Mary and Mama were listening, but then Daddy just interrupted me like I wasn't talking. He said something to Ben about taking the garbage out or something. I said, "Hey, I was talking here." He got mad and told me not to be disrespectful. Which I guess I was, but my daddy isn't usually like that.

Mama said real nicely to him that he did actually interrupt me. Then he got really mad and just left the table. He went downstairs and we didn't see him the rest of the night. Ben told me later to just let him be. Usually when one of us gets annoyed or angry we have been taught to go make things right with the other person. My parents do this with us and we are supposed to do this with others. But not this time. He never said anything to me about it and that's pretty weird. Ben says not to worry about it. I do feel worried, though.

Chapter 26: From Ricky's Journal

I can tell Mama is plenty worried about him, too. Mama says he is depressed and working through his grief. I don't know why he can't work through whatever it is and still be normal, but I guess that is how it is with depression. I used to love being at home, but lately I haven't been wanting to be around anyone else either. My room has become my favorite place instead of the kitchen where I usually hang out.

I feel all weird inside, too. Used to be, if I couldn't talk to Mama (and because of the situation with Daddy, I can't) or Dad (and obviously, I can't talk to him) I would talk to Uncle Mike. So this is where my problem kicks in. I haven't got anyone to talk to. And I am starting to worry myself. Mama says I have been moping around. I'm just starting to feel like nothing matters.

I haven't felt like doing much, not even running. Tennis is going to start soon and I haven't even played much to get ready. I just don't have the energy. Finally, the other day, I started talking to Emily about everything. I didn't want to talk about it, but she actually asked me what was wrong. It felt good that someone even noticed something might be wrong.

When Emily asked me what was going on, I told her, "Nothing." But she pointed out how much I have been isolating myself and not wanting to go places. She said she'd noticed both Daddy and I weren't running like we usually did. So I told her how this gloominess hangs over the house, and how lifeless I feel. I have never felt like this before and to be honest it scares me.

It's been three months since the funeral and Daddy is still distant and depressed. I don't know why it bothers me so much. Ben doesn't even seem to notice. But I feel it whenever I am home and especially whenever Daddy is around. If he is talking to us at all it just seems like it is because he's cranky and doesn't like something we did.

Emily said she noticed it, too. She said she has even been praying about it with some friends at church. I was surprised. I hadn't thought about praying about it with her or anyone. I think there is something about this thing with Daddy that scares me so much I can't really articulate it to anyone, even God. Emily helped me because she reminded me to talk it all over with God. So I started that night writing how I was feeling and trying to tell God about it.

Emily and Mama both say we have to give Daddy time. Emily said she had talked to our older sister, Hope, and Hope told her that when her mama died (Daddy's first wife, Kris) it took him a while to get back to normal. Hope said she would pray for him. She asked if we had talked to Mom about it. Emily told her she had talked to Mama.

Chapter 26: From Ricky's Journal

It made me feel a little better to talk to my sister, but it sure doesn't make it any easier to be his kid in this house right now. Emily told me she wishes he would snap out of it, too. She said she really needs his help with things going on with her career. She said she knows it is selfish when he is the one hurting. I think she has a point. I mean, he is the dad. And me, Ben, Mama, and all of us, really need him.

Em said, "I moved back home because I wasn't doing too good out on the road. I felt like Daddy could really help me. But, man, he hasn't offered so much as a word of advice these past couple of months!" I know what she means.

Anyway, I feel better about it since I talked with Emily and now I know Hope and Beth know too. My big sisters are really cool. I think I will talk to Mama, too. Ben said he doesn't want to talk about it. I know he hates thinking about stuff he can't control. He just tells me not to bug Dad and quit worrying so much. But it makes me anxious and I can't just stop being anxious. I sure hope something changes soon. I feel like I'm falling apart here.

CHAPTER 27
Praying for Daylight

"That's got a nice clean sound. We'll dress it up more later, but it will work for now." Nate gave Emily the green light to start with the next song. "Your voice has a lot of character and sounds great recorded." Nate, a friend of Tina's brother, was young and edgy. He had a good ear for raw talent and he'd worked hard to convince Emily and her agent to give his studio a chance.

Rachel and Tina were spending the day with Emily in Nashville. Emily had invited the women to come with her as she recorded a few songs for her new album. It had been a while since Rachel had been in Nashville and sat through a recording session. She had never been in this small studio, but she was enjoying its quiet cozy feel.

Rachel had been with TJ a couple of times when he recorded. He still did a song every now and again for a benefit or with other artists. TJ never minded having Rachel or the kids tag along. The boys had been about nine and ten the last time. But the studios TJ used with his whole band were large. Rachel had even been with Tina a few times during recording. She loved being part of the process and watching this side of their trade.

Today it was just the three of them, a ladies day out. The band wasn't even there. It was just Emily and her guitar. Emily's producer and her new agent had encouraged her to record some of her early songs, ones she wrote while she was in school. These were songs she had played when she first started singing in bars and for family and friends. Trying to make it big, she had somehow moved away from her own songs to those written by others. This was the Emily that Rachel remembered.

Tina and Rachel were allowed to be in the control booth with Nate while he worked with Emily on getting just the right blend through the recording equipment. Tina, with all her experience, had additional insights about the process. Rachel was enjoying the songs Emily had written, her simple songs of faith, family and down-home roots.

She hadn't seen her daughter play and sing in what seemed like ages. The songs brought back memories. Because Emily had written them, she had shared their meaning. Rachel could remember exactly what was going on in their lives when Emily had created each one. A new song caught her attention as Emily's smooth, rich voice rang true.

She couldn't go home and

She couldn't walk away

Chapter 27: *Praying for Daylight*

There was confusion and there was pain

But there was hope and there was faith

She was counting on love

She was counting on grace

Not knowing what would happen

But sure to find her place

"She is really good," Tina said quietly to Rachel. "I like this much better than the stuff she has been doing."

Rachel couldn't answer. She was crying. Tina saw she was overcome with emotion and patted her hand. Rachel nodded, smiling through the tears. It touched her deeply to hear Emily's words, a view of her heart Rachel hadn't seen in so long. The words to Emily's latest song spoke about the depth of trust in her dad, and her difficult decision to come home. It was a song she had written after Mike's death and how she saw her family pull together even when things were dark and difficult.

Since the funeral three months earlier there had been a remarkable change in Emily. The first was that she started communicating with the family more. She closed the distance, moving in with her sister Beth, but also by making an effort to text or call each day. Not only was she in touch with Rachel more, Emily started checking in with her brothers and sisters, and especially with TJ, too.

Another remarkable change was asking TJ and Tina for advice, or at least their opinions. Before, she had been adamant about not needing their help, but she had softened and she wanted to do things differently. She was even going to church with them again.

To anyone else, these changes may have seemed small, but Rachel knew they signaled the beginning of a new season for Emily. There was a positive shift. Though TJ had not seemed to take much notice, it made Rachel happy.

Since TJ was less available, Emily had been spending more time with Tina. For Tina it could not have come at a better time. She was still grieving, missing Mike very much and feeling alone. Emily's sudden interest in her musical talents and expertise was just what she needed to keep from getting stuck in her own loss and pain.

Emily motioned for Tina and Rachel to come down from the control room into the live booth. "Aunt Tina!" Emily was practically giddy when they got there. She was waving a song sheet like a flag. "This song—we've done it together a few times at home. Would you sing it with me?"

"Oh Honey, I don't know." Tina looked flattered, but flustered. "I'm retired, you know. I'm not sure—"

Chapter 27: *Praying for Daylight*

"Please?" Emily begged. She looked pleadingly at Rachel. "Tell her, Mom. It would mean so much to me."

Rachel put her hand on Tina's back. "What would it hurt?" she asked, giving her friend a small nudge. Tina thought a moment longer and then agreed. She said it would probably be cut from the album anyway.

Rachel went back to the control room to listen. She could not stop smiling. There was something special about seeing Emily and Tina singing together. It just felt right. It brought back a flood of memories of Emily, TJ, Tina and their friends singing around campfires at the farm or at Mike and Tina's. She and Mike would always sit next to each other and he would tease her, saying they were the real talent of the crew, then he would try to harmonize with her. She would, of course, tease him right back. "Well, Mike, I can tell you never sang in church much."

Suddenly a new wave of longing for Mike, last summer and TJ hit her and suddenly she was aware of how long it had been since she had such a good, happy day. Last summer seemed like it was years ago. Was it just last July at the Metcafe's annual fourth of July party when she and Mike had stood shoulder to shoulder watching Emily, Tina and TJ sing on the backyard make-shift stage?

The past few months had been so extremely difficult.

The boys had settled back into school. All the guests had gone home. The older kids were back to their regular lives and Tina was trying to pick up the pieces of her life. TJ was home a lot these days but very distant. Emily had been a bright spot with her enthusiasm and freshly renewed faith. Rachel coped by staying busy, not that she really had to try. Between clients, checking on Tina and the boys' activities she had plenty to keep her occupied.

Christmas had been a blur. Tina decided to take Laney to Europe and spend Christmas with Annie. Having spent so much time since Mike's passing with Tina, Rachel had to admit she felt a little lost without her. TJ, who was usually such great company was certainly the gloomiest Rachel had ever seen. Even with the grandkids around it had been difficult to elicit smiles or play time with TJ.

TJ, who was usually the most jovial and fun at Christmas, was struggling more than words could express. He had none of his usual holiday spirit. It was difficult to entice him from the dark place he was in. He tried at times to show interest in family activities, but he wasn't fooling anyone. He was still visibly hurting from the loss of his best friend.

Throughout winter the boys were home more. Come February, conditioning for spring sports would begin. Ricky was waiting for tennis in the spring. Ben was slowly climbing out of the hole he had dug for himself during the fall semester. He had wanted to play basketball, but his grades were still lacking and so he was not eligible. Rachel was somewhat relieved they had a little more time before the next run of sports. With everyone hanging out closer to home, Ben seemed content to wait until baseball season, and he was working diligently to get his grades up. While Ricky seemed to be as mopey as TJ through the winter, Ben was doing well at home and at school.

TJ typically coached at least one of the kids' teams and played on an "old guys" baseball team in the spring. But at the end of February, when the coaches met for Heritage teams, TJ told Rachel he was taking a break from coaching and playing this spring. While it had made sense he wasn't coaching basketball, Rachel worried about TJ's lack of interest in the things he generally loved to spend time doing.

By the time March rolled around, Ben was ready to play. Sitting around all winter, working on school work rather than basketball, he was eager to get out of the house and engage in sports. It was encouraging to Rachel that Ben was ready to be on a team again. But her concern for TJ was growing with each passing day.

Not only did TJ spend the winters helping out with basketball at the high school, working on spring and summer planning for Hope Enterprises, he was often out fishing whenever he could sneak away for a few hours. When the girls were all at home TJ would joke about winter being long and hard on him with all the women in the house. This winter, though, TJ was downhearted, taking naps, and yet had a restlessness about him. He seldom went to the office and only checked in with Tucker as necessary. Most concerning was the overall lack of the excitement and zeal he almost always brought with him.

Rachel did what she could, picking up some of the slack by handling school issues with the boys and fielding questions from the older kids about how their dad was doing. She had confided in Tina very little. Tina had her own battles with grief and life changes and her own decisions to weigh in on. Rachel did not want Tina to also worry about TJ. As Rachel watched Tina laughing and joking with Emily, she realized how much she had missed simple laughter, music and fun. Today was good medicine for Rachel. It felt great to be out of the house and not worrying about how everyone was doing.

After the recording, Emily and Tina wanted to go out to lunch at the small Mexican restaurant where Rachel and her girls had met TJ for the first time. It was a family favorite, and was fairly quiet when they caught it just right.

Emily was bubbling with excitement about the new album and how awesome Tina sounded. Tina was all smiles, happier than Rachel had seen her in a long while. Rachel

Chapter 27: *Praying for Daylight*

watched and listened to the two as they talked about music. She sat back, not having to be fully engaged fully. She was able to relax and just be part of their joy.

"Hey Rache." Tina was studying her, pulling her out of her own thoughts. Rachel realized her mind had been far away. "Rache, how are the boys and TJ doing?" Rachel looked at her friend and then to her daughter. Emily gave her a nod of consent to speak openly.

"The kids, all of them, seem to be doing really well. Ben is getting caught up with school and talking about baseball this spring. His counselor has helped him to process the day at the pond with Mike. I think Ben is coming through it probably the best really and certainly better than I expected. Mary is working down at Hope Center and she and Tucker have actually been seeing a lot of one another. I have high hopes about actually about that young man and Mary. I am really happy to have Emily home more. Today was just remarkable."

Rachel patted Emily's knee. "Em, it makes me so happy to hear you sing like you did today. I am glad to hear your own songs and see the light in your eyes again."

Emily nodded and smiled. "It was a long, hard way home. But I am glad I found out I could come back." Suddenly serious, she added, "But Mom, you have to tell Aunt Tina about Daddy." Her face showed the same deep concern Rachel felt. If she had wondered how much the kids picked up on, Emily's face gave it all away.

Rachel took a deep breath, tears springing to her eyes. "Oh, it has just been such a tough winter for TJ."

Tina leaned forward "What? Why haven't you said anything?" She looked from Rachel to Emily. "Never mind, I know why." Of course, Tina realized she'd been trying to shield her from any further stress. Since she'd walked this path of pain with TJ before, Tina knew what to ask. "Is he hiding out? Sulking around the house? I bet he isn't doing much, is he?"

Rachel nodded. She wasn't sure what to say.

"When Kris died he was the same way. Mike had to drag him back into life."

"Yeah, well, I haven't been able to do that," Rachel said grimly. "He does what is required, but honestly, Tina, I don't know the person he is right now. At all. I get it—I know he is depressed. He is mourning. That is a good word for it. He probably has post-traumatic stress from Mike's death. He won't go to the pond at all. He's irritable and when he does sleep, he has nightmares."

Rachel was surprised how good it felt to tell someone how difficult it had been. "He tells me very little about what he

Chapter 27: Praying for Daylight

is thinking or feeling. If he were my client I am sure I could get him to open up, but he isn't my client, he is my husband. Honestly, most days I don't know if I should push him, just let him be, or how much to even put up with."

The words just came tumbling out. Rachel forgot about being sensitive to Tina or guarding Emily from hearing their troubles. She described his moodiness and how they were all walking on eggshells. She expressed her worries, and as she did, her own grief came out. She confessed how exhausted she felt trying to hold the family together. Emily added details here and there.

When the food came, Rachel finally stopped and wiped her checks. She noticed Tina doing the same.

"Rache, you should have told me all this before."

"I didn't want to burden you, Tina. I know—"

"Nonsense, girl. You are my sister. We are supposed to go through this together. Look, I know that you know TJ way better than I do, but trust me, I have seen him like this before. And I'm telling you all, I have seen him worse." She chortled at some memory. "I knew if I introduced the two of you there was going to be a time when I was going to have to help you handle that man." She laughed again. "Kind of surprised you haven't needed me before. Mike used to give TJ a hard time, teasing him about being a full time job to manage." Tina reached across the table and put her hand on Rachel's. "I am just sorry I haven't been able to help you sort this out."

"Well, I actually feel a little better. I mean, just remembering you all have seen him through this before gives me hope. And yes, I sure could use your help. Where in the world have you been?" Rachel rolled her eyes at her friend. They both cracked up.

"Well, I sure hope if I ever get married the two of you will help me out," Emily laughed along with them.

"Sure, sugar. Just bring him on over to Aunt Tina. We'll get him all straightened out." It wasn't really funny, but it sent them all off laughing again. Rachel wiped away tears, hoping to get enough control over her laughter so she could eat. But as soon as they stopped giggling someone would say something that set them off again.

"We are going to get thrown out of here, y'all," Tina said. But Rachel could see how wonderful this day had been for all of them. Finally, they regained control and the conversation shifted again to more serious matters.

"You know, Tina, TJ and I have often joked that it took four people to make our marriage work: you, me, TJ and Mike. Maybe TJ isn't sure how to move forward without that constant support."

Chapter 27: *Praying for Daylight*

"What about you, Rache? How are you doing with moving on?" Tina asked with all the sincerity of a true best friend.

Rachel was able to share her struggles, mostly her constant anxiety, about how everyone else was doing. She missed Mike, but her worry about the others' feelings overshadowed everything else.

"That's how I was when Kris passed. I was so worried about my kids, TJ and especially his girls I didn't have time to really miss my best friend. Once TJ started doing better and I could see he was going to take care of those kids I sort of fell apart. But I had my family and career, and of course, I had Mike. We all limped through it just like we are now."

They nibbled at their food. None of them was in a hurry to get home. Rachel felt lighter just resting in the comfort of sharing her feelings and being supported by Tina.

Emily shared the impact of Laney's comments at the funeral about her dad, how he was really her stepfather, but yet he had been the only daddy she had ever known. It made her realize how much TJ meant to her and their family. Emily hadn't told Rachel the inner struggle she'd had on the road or what had turned her around. Rachel had noticed the changes, but they hadn't talked about the path Emily had been on.

"Uncle Mike's passing brought me home," Emily said.

"He helped me get away from where I was headed and Laney helped me to see how much I had at home."

"That's Mike for you," Tina said. "He's still helping people."

Rachel agreed. Everyone was quiet a moment, thinking about the impact of one man's life that reached even beyond the grave.

Tina said it was tough at the ranch without him. Annie would be coming back soon. Tina feared even with Annie home, it would still be much too big and too empty for them.

"Have you thought about selling the ranch?" Emily asked.

"Actually, I have. But this grief group I am going to told us not to make any big decisions for the first year. I have talked to Laney and Annie about it, but we are going to wait and see how we feel about it in the fall."

Rachel nodded. Emily leaned across the table toward Tina.

"Why don't you come sing with me this summer? I don't have a lot on the schedule. My agent is booking some venues closer to home. I just kind of dropped out of sight these last few months while I have been trying to get my life back together. But I bet we could talk to my agent, and—and my dad could pull a few strings, too."

Chapter 27: *Praying for Daylight*

Emily started talking faster. Tina held up her hand to stop her.

Laughing, Tina said, "Hold on a second there. First, I still have my own strings I could pull if I wanted to. And second, you aren't the first one to have that idea. But I am retired, you know. And I am probably too old for your crowd."

Rachel and Emily both disagreed with her on that last part, knowing full well many long-time award-winning artists went out on the road with young singers all the time. In fact, Alan Jackson was touring that very minute with a singer/songwriter who had once been his waitress at his favorite diner in Nashville.

"Well, would you at least consider it?" Emily asked. True to her style, she wasn't going to let go of a good idea easily.

"Tell you what," Tina said after a thoughtful pause. "I will consider it. But only because I had so much fun singing with you today." Then she added, "And because your Uncle Mike actually suggested something along those lines back when you were giving us all such cause for worry."

"Really?" Rachel and Emily asked at the same time.

Tina laughed at their jinx. "Yeah, really. So out of respect for Mike I will consider it. Just keep in mind, I am not promising anything."

Tina wouldn't allow any further conversation about her possible come-back career. Instead, she asked about baseball, Ricky's tennis matches, and the Keyton grandkids. Rachel and Emily knew when she said she would think about it later there was no need for pressure. She would.

Wrapping up the meal, the conversation turned again to TJ.

"Rache, I know you don't think it will do any good, but I'm telling you, with TJ and this depression he is in you gotta get in there and push him."

"But—"

"I know. He is stubborn. He will push right back. You have no idea how hard I had to push to get him to do anything, including coming to meet you right here in this same restaurant way back in the day."

Rachel decided not to argue. She contemplated this new information. She hadn't ever thought about their "chance meeting" in terms of how many strings Tina had pulled to make it happen. The TJ she knew saw opportunities and took them without hesitation. When he didn't want to do something, though, she knew he could hold his ground just as solid.

She sighed heavily. "I don't know, Tina. It hasn't been my

role to make TJ do anything. I keep thinking he just needs time and space. I have suggested your grief group, even counseling for his PTSD symptoms. I can't even get him to go fishing right now. So you are saying to just make him? How? How do I do that?"

"Honey, you've got a lot more leverage than Mike and I had." She winked. "I know you can figure it out. One thing for sure. We learned you can't let him sit and withdraw too long. At first we thought, like you said, give him time and space and he'll come around. But for whatever reason, TJ needed us to go into his dark place and drag him out. Make him play catch with Ben, take the boys fishing, go to counseling. If all else fails, make him come see me. You know nobody will make him talk about Mike more than me. Use whatever you have to, Rache."

"Yeah—" Rachel was turning this over in her mind. She thought of a list of things she wanted to see TJ do again and wondered how hard she would have to push.

Turning to Emily, Tina said, "Yep. And I will think over your offer, miss." They stood and started for the door. "It's a new season for us all."

CHAPTER 28
Heart Like a Sad Song

Rachel stood by the big family calendar hanging in the kitchen. It was a huge white board TJ had converted into a monthly schedule that could be erased or added to as needed. Rachel was realizing, as she looked over the activities, they hadn't had a real family meeting in months, a lot of months. In the past, family meetings had been weekly.

TJ had started them with his kids and brought Rachel and her girls in on the meetings as soon as they had moved to Tennessee. When the boys had first come home the family meetings were regular events. But through the years the meetings had become less frequent.

This was due in part to fewer children at home, but the real reason was the boys made those meetings extremely difficult. Ben, in particular, was nearly impossible in group meetings even with family. He was disruptive or he would sulk. Ricky also had a hard time but his was with sitting quietly and listening without monopolizing the conversation or taking over the meeting with his silliness.

If there were more than a couple of the girls present the meetings often ended in some kind of meltdown. There was a time when Rachel dreaded those family meetings. When they were working on getting the boys' behaviors under control they switched the format to family activity time. That allowed Rachel and TJ to work with the boys on social language skills, social behaviors and positive family interactions.

By the time the boys hit junior high, TJ had implemented more of a monthly check-in. They sometimes Skyped with whoever was away. It became a time to touch base with the girls and their families and make plans for visits, bigger events or other activities. Then they'd record their plans on the calendar. Rachel also kept an electronic version that all the family could access on their mobile devices.

Since Mike had passed, TJ did not seem to have the energy to keep up with everyone's comings and goings. Rachel did her best to update the calendar, but TJ had lost interest in what everyone was doing. Even going over plans or ideas at dinner seemed to fall on deaf ears. His mind was elsewhere, and Rachel wasn't sure what he was thinking about, but there was no mistaking his withdrawal.

Rachel thought about Tina's advice to push him to do normal things, but she wasn't sure where to start. This morning as she packed lunches and checked the schedule for Ben's baseball practices and Rick's tennis matches, the idea of calling a family meeting came to her.

Chapter 28: Heart Like a Sad Song

Rarely did she call these meetings. She usually left that to TJ. But she added "Family Meeting" to the calendar for after dinner Wednesday night.

Rachel finished the lunches as TJ came into the kitchen.

"Hey Babe." She greeted him with a kiss. He turned slightly so she kissed his check. He didn't stay close enough for a hug. She tried not to sigh. She missed his happy morning self that used to welcome each day with enthusiasm and her with warmth.

She handed him a cup of coffee. He lingered near the counter looking off in the distance. She studied him. His hair seemed to be graying more every day. The stress and sorrow of the past couple months were etched in his face. Rachel didn't look away when he turned and saw her staring.

"What?"

She shook her head and gave him a tender smile. "Nothing. You're just a sight for sore eyes." She dried her hands on the towel and proceeded to wrap her arms around his waist. "I sure miss your kisses in the morning."

He didn't pull away. He held her close and kissed the top of her head. She could feel his heart beating through his flannel shirt and smelled hay and cologne. It was familiar and comforting.

"I know," he said softly into her hair. "I'm sorry."

She waited, quiet. She was afraid to even hint at pulling back. Tender moments had been sporadic these past months, usually only if she initiated them. A few times he had reached for her late at night when he couldn't sleep. As Rachel leaned against him TJ ran his hand over her hair. He caressed her cheek with the back of his fingers then gently lifted her chin and looked directly into her eyes.

A thousand questions raced through her mind. She wanted to ask him why he had been so aloof. Did he know how rare this moment was? How could she help? Why was he suddenly paying attention to her? She feared he would see her hesitation and misinterpret it. But instead he leaned down and kissed her tenderly with a hint of wanting. Hungry for him, she returned his kiss eagerly. Her questions were gone and for a moment things felt right and normal. She wanted to lose herself in the passion she felt and forget her worrying for him.

TJ pulled back with a chuckle and a small groan. He ran his hand through his short hair and shook his head. "Damn girl."

She pressed against him. "Let's forget about today." She took his hand as if to lead him back to the bedroom. But they both knew it was impossible. Already she could hear the boys getting ready for the day. Music blared upstairs and

Chapter 28: Heart Like a Sad Song

Mary was sure to bounce into the house any moment.

"I wish," TJ chuckled. He looked at her for a moment. Rachel returned the gaze. How long had it been since he had really seen her? She considered the possibility he might come through this grieving on his own after all. But already she could feel the depression creeping in again. The constant sadness lingered in his eyes. These days he was like a turtle. It never took much for him to duck back into his shell.

It was time to shift gears. "TJ, I am thinking we should have a family meeting this week."

He looked surprised and instantly resistant. "Why? What's going on?"

"Nothing. We just haven't had one all winter, and spring is already getting busy with sports and school ending before long. I was thinking Wednesday night we could all attempt to get on the same page."

He didn't look eager, but at least he agreed it was a good idea. Rachel sighed inwardly with relief. Now she just needed to talk to the kids about her idea.

CHAPTER 29
If I Didn't Have You

Wednesday night, after the dinner dishes had been cleared, the boys, Rachel and Mary sat in the front room with TJ. It was tradition to have dessert during the meetings. Keeping in step with custom, Rachel had provided all the fixings for ice cream sundaes. She called them back to the kitchen to create their own.

Once everyone had settled into their spots with their desserts, Rachel sat on the edge of her chair expectantly. TJ typically started the meetings, but he gave Rachel the go ahead with a simple nod of his head. It was, after all, her assembly.

Rachel cleared her throat. She noted it had been a while since they'd had a real family meeting. She said she was sorry and she knew it had been a difficult winter for all of them. The kids were listening, and they agreed.

"TJ, Babe—" She turned to her husband. "—it seems it has been extremely difficult for you. We are all worried about you. I wanted to have this meeting for each of us to say how much we love you, but also how much we need you, and especially how much we want to help you, because of all of us, it seems you are struggling the most."

"I wouldn't go that far," TJ protested.

Rachel signaled for Mary to begin.

"Daddy, I want to read something I wrote for you. I hope you will give us all a chance to share with you." She looked to him for approval. Mary was his youngest daughter and there was no way he could tell her no to sharing her feelings.

He drew a deep breath and nodded.

Mary set her bowl aside and unfolded a paper she pulled from her jeans pocket. She swallowed hard, pushing back tears.

"All my life, you have been strong for me. You have been my hero, my Daddy-the-invincible. When Mama died, I was so little, but I remember you being sad. I remember I was worried about you being lonely, but you were still so big and strong for us girls. Without Mama here, you became my everything. Daddy. You have been the most constant thing in my life besides God. I count on you more than you probably know.

Daddy, I know you are sad now because of Uncle Mike's passing. I was thinking maybe all that time you had to be tough for us when Mama died is adding to your sadness. And maybe all your pain is making it really hard for you to be

Chapter 29: If I Didn't Have You

around us right now. Because it seems like you are pushing us all away. For the first time in my life, I feel like you are not here for me, for us. I don't know how to help you feel better, but I think maybe you just need to know that I still need you, we all do. Daddy, please get help so we can all heal and move forward."

Rachel had been watching TJ during Mary's letter. He had kept his head down, emotions in check. He fiddled with his ring and he didn't look up until Mary was done. She walked over to him and he stood and gave her a hug. He leaned down and whispered something in her ear. Mary kissed him on the cheek and then sat down on the couch by her brothers.

TJ didn't sit. He turned and looked at Rachel. His eyes were dark. It was easy to see she had taken him off guard.

"Is this what this is about?" he asked accusingly.

Rachel started to defend herself and her decision to approach TJ in this manner. But then Ricky stood up.

"Daddy, I want to read my letter to you, too. Please?"

TJ gave Rachel a disapproving look before he turned his attention to Rick. Ricky looked worried, vulnerable. Rachel breathed a sigh of relief when TJ met him with gentleness.

"Of course you can." He looked at each of the kids as he wiped his hands on his Wranglers. "You all can read what you wrote to me. But I am not going to lie, this is very uncomfortable for me. I can't say I like it. I really don't. But I want to know what you have on your minds. Of course I do."

He sat down and nodded to Ricky. "Go ahead, Son."

"When Uncle Mike died, I didn't think I could make it past all the sadness in this house. Everyone was crying and there was just so much grief all around. It hurt knowing Aunt Tina and her family were so unhappy, and I hated seeing you and Mama crying and just all of us so sad. It was overwhelming. I felt like a big dark blanket had been pulled over my head and a ton of bricks were sitting on my chest. I had never felt so miserable in my life.

I hadn't thought much about death or dying before that day. I didn't think anyone close to me was going to die for a long time. Now I know it can happen in a moment and I am still afraid of who is going to be next. Sometimes at night I can't sleep because I start thinking about who will die and what will happen. My chest feels tight and I can't breathe. I feel tired all the time and I can't concentrate. I think it's because I hate going to bed. I stay up in my room and read a lot.

For a long time now I wanted to talk to you about it, but I couldn't. So when Mama said we could write a letter to you about what it has been like for us since Uncle Mike died and

Chapter 29: If I Didn't Have You

what we wanted you to know, I was glad to finally get to tell you.

The stuff I think about that keeps me awake is pretty awful and I wish you could help me get through my own fears. I know it isn't encouraging, and it probably isn't going to help you feel better, so maybe this isn't what I should write. But Daddy, here's the thing. Ever since I met you, ever since I came to this family, when I was scared I could trust you. Believe me, I was scared a lot when I was little, maybe more than you know. But you and Mama would be there for me.

I could talk to Mama and she helped me to feel loved and cared for, but Daddy, you made me not afraid. You would come near me and even when I couldn't understand why I felt so lousy I knew I was going to be okay because you were close. When I got older, I depended on the strength of this family to be there for me even when I was afraid, or mad or hurt. Even though I have been really scared about dying, I have been more scared about what is happening with you,

Daddy. I know you are really sad, and maybe like me, you are scared. I am okay because I have this family, but I need you. I need you, Daddy, to help me not be so afraid. I just wanted you to know. I love you."

Rachel felt sheepish. She'd had no idea the extent of Ricky's fears or struggles. It moved TJ as well. He was sitting in a big overstuffed chair, but he scooted over and gestured for Rick to come sit with him. When the boys were young Rachel or TJ would sit in that chair with them and read to them or have connecting time. Ricky, almost fourteen and lanky, was partly on TJ's lap as he snuggled in. TJ put his arm around him and held him tightly. Even after they hugged, TJ kept his arm around Rick's shoulders. There wasn't a dry eye in the room except for Ben's. He was fidgeting, anxiously awaiting his turn.

Without any fanfare or pretense, Ben stood, cleared his throat and started his letter.

"Daddy, I hope you can hear everything I am wanting to say and I hope in this moment I can say everything I want you to hear.

So many times when I was stuck in my fear and my own kind of grief, which looked an awful lot like anger, you stood with me. You held me, you walked with me, and you helped me keep moving forward. Maybe it takes one to know one, but when I see you these days I keep thinking you are stuck just like I was.

Daddy, I wish I could help you feel better about Uncle Mike, but I can't. No one can. You have to let him go. And you have to stop blaming yourself. Remember you told me this about my old life? That I had to let go and stop looking

Chapter 29: If I Didn't Have You

back so I could move forward. Now, I guess it is my turn to tell you. But even more than telling you to move on, I want to tell you I need you. Mama needs you, Aunt Tina needs you. So do the girls and so does my little brother.

Instead of thinking about how sad you are, how mad you are at God for taking your best friend, you have to let it go and embrace what you have here. We are family, and you taught me that means we stand together. We are with you. We will walk with you and help you to move forward in any way we can but you gotta let us help."

Ricky wiggled around, moving so TJ could get up. First, TJ gave Ben a firm handshake, but then he pulled him gruffly into a hug. Turning toward the group, TJ gave Rachel a long look. He seemed to be contemplating what to say.

"Do you have something to say as well?" he asked. He no longer sounded angry.

"Not right now." Rachel could see he was ready to talk and there was clearly nothing more she could add to what the kids had already said. Emily was away for the evening, but she had written a letter as well. Rachel fingered it in her jean pocket, but decided to let TJ read it on his own later. Maybe this was enough for now.

TJ looked carefully at each of them. There was a tenderness in his eyes, a warmth Rachel hadn't seen in a while. He fiddled with his ring, and then shoved his hands into his pockets. He didn't say anything for a moment.

Rachel felt a flood of emotions. He looked so vulnerable, and TJ never was vulnerable. Something in his fragility evoked the deepest feelings Rachel had for him. It played on her feelings of love, respect and compassion.

TJ chose to sit down before he spoke. "Well," he started. "That is about as close to an intervention as I have ever seen." He paused and cleared his throat. The family waited.

"Funny thing is, a long time ago, Mike, Tina and Mary's mama, sat me down and gave me a 'what for' talkin' to similar to—but even more intense—than this one. Back then it was about my drinkin' and how I was throwing my life away. I needed it then, and I guess I needed it tonight." TJ toyed with his ring again. Everyone was quiet.

"One thing for sure, I know Mike would'a thought it was a good idea." TJ was thoughtful. He looked up at his family. Rachel was surprised at the tears in his eyes. "I'm not trying to hurt any of you." He swallowed hard and rubbed his hand over the scruff of his unshaven face. "But I can see I have been. And I am sorry about that."

No one said anything for a while. Each was lost in his or her own thoughts. Rachel finally broke the silence.

Chapter 29: If I Didn't Have You

"It's been a long tough winter for all of us. No one wanted to make you feel worse. We love you and we know you love us. We have all needed time to work through our grief and loss. But then it seemed like the more space we gave you, the more distant you became. And I miss you, Babe. We all do."

TJ nodded. "I don't know what you all hope will happen after tonight. And I wish I had an answer for you. I don't. I feel stuck, I do. I'm frustrated with that. I am angry, too. Angry that people I care about die around me and I can't do anything about it. If I am really honest, maybe I am a little mad at God about that one. Having been through this before, I kind of figured that if I could just give it time I would start to feel better. Time heals all wounds, right? But I haven't been feeling better. That's for sure."

He looked at the faces around the room. Then he focused on Rachel. "Thanks for having the courage to call me on the carpet. I am sorry. I bet it wasn't an easy decision to make. Did Tina tell you to do it?" Rachel laughed and shook her head.

"Not in so many words. She just encouraged me to do everything I could to pull you out of this funk you are in."

"I wish I could just pull myself out. I do. But I do I promise to do what is necessary to get better. Okay? And I guess I am going to need to get some help to work through all this crap in my head."

Rachel laughed, "Well, my love, you have come to the right place."

"Really? You know a shrink?"

It had been a long time since Rachel had seen them all laugh together or engage like this. She didn't want it to end. But it was getting late. Ricky said he needed some help with a homework assignment. Ben asked if they were done and excused himself to take a shower and get ready for bed. Mary gave everyone a hug and then practically skipped off to her little cottage.

Later that night, for the first time in months, TJ came into the bedroom to seek Rachel out. It had become his habit to watch TV or hang out in his office until long after she had gone to bed. Most nights Rachel would get ready for bed and then find him to say goodnight or try to entice him to bed. Tonight he came in behind her as she was brushing her teeth. He wrapped his arms around her. She quickly rinsed her mouth, then turned to find him smiling at her.

"Hey," he said, somewhat sheepishly.

"Hey, yourself," she smiled. "What's up?"

"Well, I was thinking about a couple things. One is that you probably had more to say to me than what you could say

Chapter 29: If I Didn't Have You

with the kids there. And two, I was thinking about what you started in the kitchen the other morning."

"Really?" Rachel couldn't resist teasing him. "You think an offer made in the morning is still good at night? Especially days later?"

He leaned down and kissed her. Rachel responded naturally. When she pulled away, he winked at her. "Guess so," he said cunningly.

"Okay, you got me," she admitted. He led her to their bed, undressed her longingly then slipped out of his own clothes. They made love slowly. It was tender and sweet. Rachel's desire was matched by TJ's passion. She savored the time as if he were a cool cup of water on a hot summer day.

"Babe?" she said afterward, as they lay in each other's arms.

"Hmm?" TJ murmured.

She rose to her elbow to look at his face to see if he was awake. His arms around her, he lightly stroked her hair. She loved lying there with him, wrapped in his arms, nothing between them. "You were right. I did have something to say to you tonight. I was hoping we would have some time like this so I could tell you."

TJ scooted up a little to let her know he was listening. "Go on," he said.

Rachel took a deep breath. She had written it all down, but she didn't want to interrupt the moment by getting it. She knew what she wanted to say, what she felt she needed to say. She gazed at TJ, overwhelmed with love and emotion. He waited.

"Well," Rachel started. "First, I wanted to say how much I love you. How much I need you. How much I miss you." She stroked his arm as she continued. "Babe, I can see what you went through with Kris as I watch you now grieving so hard with your loss of Mike. Clearly, it haunts you. But I wanted to say, you can't control who lives, or who dies. I think you are really scared. Maybe more so than you have ever been. Mike's death really jolted you. Maybe now you are afraid to care too much, even about all of us, maybe about life. But, TJ, I don't want to live afraid of dying."

TJ rolled on his back and stared at the ceiling. Rachel could tell he was listening. She finished up her thoughts.

"I wish I could promise you, Babe—that I am not going anywhere, but you know that would be a dandelion promise. What I can promise you is that I won't let what might happen stop me from fully living every day we have. One of your favorite quotes is, 'All men die, but few men really live.' I promise, TJ, to really live. I want you to promise me you will, too."

TJ sat up and scooted his back against the headboard. Rachel sat next to him, giving him time to digest what she had said.

Finally, rubbing his chin, he said somberly, "Rache, I hear you. I really do. I wish I could tell you what is wrong with me. I wish I could just snap out of it. Be done with feeling heavyhearted, and being panicked every time someone rushes up to me to say something. It feels like the next bad thing is going to happen any minute. I am frustrated with feeling so powerless, Rache. I am sorry for not handling this better, and for letting y'all down."

Rachel moved close to him and he put his arm around her, pulling her against his bare chest. He lifted her chin. His eyes, full of sentiment, were darker than usual. In his words and through his eyes, Rachel could sense his brokenness. He didn't talk for a while. He looked in her eyes and gently stroked her hair and caressed her face.

Finally, his voice deep and raspy with emotion. "Babe, all I can promise you is what I promised the family. I promise to get help. I won't give up. But Rache, promise me, too, you won't give up on me. Even if I am a complete dumb-ass I am smart enough to know I need you. Right now, I need you to hang in there with me."

Rachel promised. More importantly, she prayed as they snuggled under the covers.

CHAPTER 30
Even If It Breaks Your Heart

Nothing happened right away. But slowly and surely the days were getting better. With a hint of summer in middle of spring, Rachel was optimistic. There were not any striking changes from the gloomy days they had battled through, but Rachel could see and sense they were coming out of the haze. As it usually is, change was found in small steps and increments measured over time rather than big moments.

After the "intervention," as TJ referred to it, he didn't recover suddenly. He did not immediately return to his former energetic, active self. During the winter he had been home more, less involved in sports and the non-profit than Rachel had ever seen him. Where once he could barely stop moving, he had practically come to a standstill. And even when spring rolled around he didn't jump into coaching again or putting a lot of irons back in the fire.

He seemed more available though. His good humor slowly returned, but he was more contemplative than he had been before. For the first time since she had met him he seemed content to watch Rick's tennis matches and watch, not coach, Ben's baseball with her. He was different—not necessarily bad— just different.

After the funeral TJ had handed over the reins to Tucker at The Hope Center and he hadn't picked them up again. Tucker and his team, which also included Mary, were doing well keeping it running and implementing new ideas for spring and summer.

At first, Rachel thought TJ would eventually return to coaching and The Hope Center. But others were willing to step in. TJ focused on the family. He slowed down. By not jumping back into the bustle of all he had been doing before, he seemed calmer. She saw he was engaged with the kids and more attentive to the atmosphere at home. She liked sitting with him at the kids' sporting events instead of watching him pace on the sidelines. And she noticed he spent more time with Rick than he had before.

Ben had always demanded more of TJ's presence. Ben was tough and strong, and at times angry and violent. When he was younger and going through his most aggressive phase TJ was habitually close at hand or on call even when Rachel was dealing with him. Things with Ben worked best when they were united and working together, and Ben needed the strength and intensity TJ offered. It had worked to keep the boys busy and structured.

In the past, the time TJ spent with Rick usually included Ben. Ricky's one-on-one time was frequently with Rachel. It was just the way it had worked out due to the difference in the boys' needs and the way they all related to one another.

Chapter 30: Even If It Breaks Your Heart

Rachel had been surprised at the depth of Rick's distress through the winter. She had not realized how Mike's death and TJ's depression had affected him. He put on a good front of being happy and everything being fine. But his letter had shown her he wasn't doing well and she was worried about him burying his sorrow. Or his grief turning inward as it did with so many kids who held in their thoughts and feelings.

After the "intervention" she got nowhere talking to him about it. He'd say, "I just want Daddy to be okay." He gave her mediocre feedback about how he was fine. He told her often that she worried too much.

She had brought this up to TJ a few times. He listened to her concerns and assured her Ricky was working through his grief. He asked her to give both him and Ricky time to process it together. It was tough for Rachel to back off with one of the kids, especially when it came to their mental and emotional well-being. But she could see TJ and Rick were connecting and she needed to move out of the way.

There was something in Ricky's letter that motivated TJ to spend more time alone with him. And now that Ben was doing better and playing baseball without TJ coaching, there was more opportunity for TJ and Ricky to build a stronger bond. Rachel regularly found TJ and Ricky hanging out downstairs or out with the horses.

Rick was a talker and he was insightful. He liked deep conversations. Although they didn't share their conversations with her, she could see a new depth in their relationship. She enjoyed watching them together. For many reasons, it made her heart happy and eased her worries.

Ben had managed to bring his grades up. He wasn't having much trouble on the baseball team. He seemed to enjoy his position at first base on the junior varsity team. He was a fair hitter and a great base runner. Overall, he was about as comfortable as Rachel had ever seen him. Maybe, she thought, he actually needed his dad to get off the field.

As the school year was ending Rachel was at peace about how things were going and the subtle changes she noticed in their family. It was definitely calmer, even with tennis. baseball, and the normal end-of-school activities. The previous seasons, especially in the fall, had been so frenzied. It felt now as though the entire family had taken a collective deep breath and were content.

Even though the progress was slow, the family was moving forward and healing. Not only with TJ and the boys but there were changes with Emily, too. She had recommitted her life to God and it was showing in everything she did. She had plans for shows that kept her close to home and she was no longer running around with her former band members and road crew. Mary was helping her get organized for the re-

Chapter 30: *Even If It Breaks Your Heart*

launch of her career. Emily seemed satisfied to keep it small and simple.

TJ had promised to get help with his grief. As a result, he'd started going with Tina to her support group each week. Rachel had worried at first it might not be enough. She asked him several times if he needed more counseling. Was he struggling with depression and posttraumatic stress disorder from witnessing Mike's death? Did Ricky need more help? But as time went on she saw he was healing, and along with him, Ricky was, too. Rachel couldn't help but feel thankful. She could see that none of them would ever be the same. Life was not going back to "normal" again (whatever that was), but they had turned a corner.

That is why it surprised her so much when TJ suddenly sprung a whole new set of plans on her. It was one of the first really warm late spring evenings. She and TJ were sitting outside on the patio talking about summer and thinking about getting the pool uncovered. Emily had been over for dinner and was challenging the boys to a game of pool downstairs. Mary was out with Tucker and two sets of grandkids were coming the next day for the weekend.

"Rache—" TJ paused, making sure he had her full attention.

Rachel heard something in his voice that drew her away

from thoughts of the goings-on with their grandchildren.

"Hmmm?"

"I'm thinkin' about going on tour this summer with Tina and Emily." He bit his lip as he waited for her response.

Rachel stared at him. It was the last thing she was expecting. He hadn't been on tour in over twelve years. Was he kidding?

"What?" she stammered. She caught a glimmer in his eyes. Though he was nervous about what she might say, clearly, he was excited. "I mean, when? When did you decide this?"

That was all the solicitation he needed. He was animated. The words, the plans, the joy he was feeling all poured out. He had been talking with Emily and a few of his old music business buddies the last couple of weeks as he helped her set up some gigs for the summer shows with Tina. The three of them had been messing around with several songs for the playlist. TJ had joined in playing guitar with Emily and singing along. He grinned lightheartedly as he told Rachel about the songs, how it felt to be involved in the music, even if it was just on the sidelines.

She watched his excitement as he shared all this with her. She tried not to show her incredulity at all the ideas and plans she had not been part of. She was torn. On one hand,

Chapter 30: Even If It Breaks Your Heart

she was happy to see his obvious elation. On the other, it hurt to not have been part of any of it.

He must have noticed her ambiguity. He looked puzzled. "You're awful quiet. What are you thinking? It's crazy, right?"

"TJ." She needed more time to consider her words. She wasn't sure how much of her feelings she should share. She was having such a difficult time understanding them herself. She was oscillating between being flabbergasted and immediately cold to the idea. She wasn't a part of the decision at all and he sounded so resolute. "I am just so surprised. It seems so sudden. But then I guess you have been planning for a while."

It was more a question than a statement. Rachel didn't want to sound so forlorn, but she felt jilted as if he were returning to a former lover.

TJ took her hand. "No, not really Babe. Like I said, I was just trying to help Emily and this took me off guard, too. You know, after I read her note to me, the one you gave me after the intervention, I decided to get more involved with mentoring her. Did you read it?"

Rachel shook her head.

"Well, remind me to show you. But it meant a lot to me.

She wrote about how she highly esteemed me as an artist way before I even met y'all. And she wrote about the hero I was to her through my music and how I lived my life. She told me she wanted my help and needed me to guide her on many levels. Anyway, I'll let you read it. But it struck a chord with me. I realized I hadn't been very available to the girls the last few years, or to Rick really, but especially not to Emily."

He was wound up, talking fast. "Some of that was due to being so caught up in sports and coaching Ben with football, basketball and baseball. I don't know. But there was something in her note which made me aware of a part of me I was missing. I spent a lot of time through the winter thinking about our life, our family and where we go from here."

He stopped, thoughtful for a moment. Rachel was struck by the transformation she saw in him.

"I think for a long while now, I was just counting on you to keep things going here at home," he continued. "You are the one that made it a soft place for any of us to land. I know you have been that for me. That made it possible for me to be all over the place and do all the stuff I was doing. That's when I realized I had been busy with a lot of doing for the kids, but not necessarily being there for them. What I heard them asking for in their notes was for me to be available on a level I wasn't." He paused to see if she was following him.

Chapter 30: *Even If It Breaks Your Heart*

Rachel nodded for him to continue.

"I realized something about my relationship with God, too. I knew I was sinking in the muck and I didn't even want to fight it. I felt a lot of shame and guilt about not being a good father, husband, or Christian. But then it hit me when I was rereading what you and the kids wrote that it wasn't about being good enough. I never was good enough. But I was loved. And somehow that got me seeing things differently. Rache, do you know, what I mean?

Rachel smiled warmly. "I do."

"After that, I felt okay being here and more at ease just hanging out with Ricky and helping Emily. You talked to me before about being present and I don't know if I really understood it. I mean, I know I am all in it whatever it is I am doing and usually that is with you or the kids. But somehow this is just different."

Rachel liked what she was hearing. It made sense with the small changes she had seen in him over the last couple months. But she didn't see how being present with the family fit with going on the road with Emily and Tina.

She said as much. "So, I'm kind of slow here because I don't see the connection between being more present at home and you leaving us to go on tour."

"I really wasn't planning going on the road. You have to understand that." He searched her face. "Rache, I don't want to jump back into all the activity I was in before, especially all the sports stuff with Ben. I want to be supportive and I want to be involved with the kids in a different way. Like the time I have been spending with Ricky. We just talk and I listen to him in a way I don't know if I ever did before. And Ben, I love cheering him on and not worrying about all the rest of the team stuff. Just being able to support him. I like being at his games and the tennis matches with you. I feel more accessible."

Rachel studied his profile in the moonlight. It was interesting how, through all his sorrow, Mike's death had helped TJ to really grow up. She could see it in his face, but more importantly, she heard it in his words.

"I've had a lot of time with God once I stopped being so busy," he said. "When I asked Him how I could help Emily, He told me not to be afraid to walk next to her. I didn't understand what He meant at first. When I read her note I thought it meant to be there for her to talk to me, to ask questions or encourage her. I realized I had done a pretty good job avoiding all that with her before. I think I was scared for her, scared of what was happening to her, and that it was my fault somehow. So I tried to help, but from a safe distance. That way no one would blame me if she kind of fell apart." He laughed at his admission.

"How did that work for you?" Rachel laughed with him.

"I know I should have talked all these things over with you. But this thing about going out with Emily this summer, it came as a surprise to me, too. Nothing is set yet. When Tina told Emily she would sing with her I wasn't part of the show at all. But when we all started rehersals and talked things over, they invited me. What surprised me was how much I wanted to do it. I discovered how much I missed the music. I couldn't believe how strongly I felt about it. I really want to do it, Rache. It's that simple." He shrugged as if there was nothing more he could say.

Something about hearing him talk like this felt good to Rachel. Too many long months of brooding depression and gloomy silence had masked their communication. They used to talk for hours about ideas, God, and the kids. How long had it been since they had planned anything new or done anything with renewed passion?

Then Rachel thought about Emily. The really big, life-altering changes they'd experienced this winter had all been with her. It was Emily who had done a 180 or maybe she had done a complete 360 and come home. Rachel considered what TJ had said about feeling responsible for Emily's fall away from God and family. She didn't know he had been praying about how to help her. Truth was, he was what helped her turn back to her faith and family. He had been the first to encourage her to sing her own songs and to keep it simple and pure. In his quietness since Mike's passing TJ had actually found a more pure, simple part of himself.

Rachel had been quiet for several minutes, mulling all this in her mind.

"Did you already tell them you would?" she wanted to know. It was the hurt part of her asking. The part that still felt left out of these ideas. There was a part of her that was afraid she would be sidelined while he went off on his own adventures. Even though she could see the positive happening, and she could feel TJ was right, there was still a sting of the new plans she felt left out of.

"No. No, Babe, it wasn't like that. I mean, seriously, nothing was that planned out. It was all sudden. They invited me yesterday morning when we were downstairs in the little studio. I prayed about it and this, right now, is the first time I have talked to anyone about it. I didn't even tell them for sure." He touched her chin, turning her head toward him. "Babe, come on. You know I wouldn't go without you. You're my team."

"It sounded like it was a done deal, the way you said it." She hoped she didn't sound accusatory.

Chapter 30: Even If It Breaks Your Heart

"I'm just really excited. I feel right about it, but I wouldn't commit to it without you."

He looked at her expectantly while she digested what he had said. He wasn't asking permission, something they had vowed not to do to each other. But he wanted her to be part of it with him. She tried to remember what it was like when he was a country star, on the road, with fans all the time. It was a vague, distant memory she could barely conjure up.

"What will it be like?" she wondered out loud. "Are you going back to being Troy Keyton?"

He laughed. "Technically, I've always been Troy Keyton."

"Oh, that's right." She laughed too. "I forgot. With, you know, Dad, Papa, TJ and, of course, all my names for you."

"Ohhh—like—"

"No, don't go there," she laughed, swatting at him teasingly. "I meant, are you going back into this fulltime? Recording, touring, screaming fans, etcetera?"

"That is not my intention. I want to go with Tina and Emily this summer. We are setting up the schedule close to home with smaller venues. I hope if we do travel more than a day or so you and the boys will join me. It's for the summer only and there are no record deals planned. Tina and I are just hoping we won't get laughed off the stage as the two oldsters who should have stayed gone."

"Oh, I doubt that. Tina is still pretty hot." Rachel laughed as he pretended to look hurt.

He shared a little more about the schedule they were working on. As dusk turned to night, Rachel was starting to feel the chill of the night air. She was still trying to wrap her mind around what the summer would be like. She had questions. When would it start? How many shows? The plans were rough, but she could feel the excitement of it.

Rachel stood to go inside, wrapping her arms around herself. "When Emily comes in the morning I hope she'll have a lot more details for me. I can see you really want to do this. And I, for one, would not stand in your way. I certainly would not want to get in Tina's way, nor Emily's for that matter. But it's hard for me to really picture it all."

She started to head into the house where it was warm. She paused by his chair. "TJ, I don't feel like I know that old part of your life. It was such a short stint of our time together back in the day when we first met. There was a time I only knew you through your music, but that seems a lifetime ago."

TJ pulled her down into his lap. He was warm and comforting.

"I was thinking," she continued, "about how God gives us opportunities to use our gifts. They don't go away even if they lie dormant for a while. You gave up the music business

Chapter 30: *Even If It Breaks Your Heart*

to help me help others and so that we could blend and build this family. Now I see we are headed into some new adventures. I'm good with that as long as we go together."

"Rache." He leaned down, turning her head, he kissed her lips. Then she leaned her head against his chest. For a moment they were still. She could feel the familiar beat of his heart and there was an overwhelming sense of being home. TJ whispered in her ear, "Thanks for standing by me. For being my soft place to land."